MAKING
FELTED FRIENDS

MAKING FELTED FRIENDS

FRIENDS

25 TOYS & GIFTS

SUE PEARL

Storey

This book is dedicated to my cat, Obi, who died just before Christmas 2006.
He was 18, had a lovely sweet nature, and always helped me when I was making my
animals. He used to sit on a cushion in my workshop while I wrapped and felted my
creatures. He is deeply missed.

The mission of Storey Publishing is to serve our customers by
publishing practical information that encourages
personal independence in harmony with the environment.

First U.S. Edition, Storey Publishing 2007

© 2007 by Breslich & Foss, Ltd.

Conceived and produced by
Breslich & Foss, Ltd.
Unit 2A, Union Court
20–22 Union Road
London SW4 6JP

Text by Sue Pearl
Photographs by Shona Wood

Library of Congress Cataloging-in-Publication Data Available Upon Request

ISBN-13: 978-1-58017-685-9

Printed in China

10 9 8 7 6 5 4 3 2 1

CONTENTS

THE PROJECTS

Introduction

It was about 12 years ago that I "discovered" felt although I was not the first, of course. Felt as a textile has a very long and noble history. Dating back 8,000 years, some say it has been credited with being the original textile, discovered before weaving and spinning.

There are many stories about the discovery of felt. These accounts usually involve a pilgrim or saint, or a sainted pilgrim, some uncomfortable footwear, a passing sheep, and a long walk. The story goes that this weary traveler is walking across the desert or mountains and places some fleece into his footwear to ease his poor aching feet. With the constant friction from walking, the sweat from his feet, and the warmth inside his shoes, the traveler has a perfect pair of felt insoles by the time he reaches his destination. I hope this story has some truth because I use it often when giving talks to groups on the history of felt!

The way I discovered felt was on a week-long course on ethnic textiles at the Victoria and Albert Museum in London. It was led by the anthropologist, Stephanie Bunn. She took us into the stores at the museum to look at the carpets, yurt covers, saddle blankets, and horse and camel head covers, all made from felt. Then, with all these wonderful objects fresh in our minds, she introduced us to the wonders of felt-making and we produced our own versions.

This was my "Eureka!" moment when I fell in love with felt. The immediacy of producing an object and decoration at the same time, and the way the wild colors mixed and worked together, all set my brain racing. The group made sample pieces, then bags, carpets, and wall hangings.

bird workshop at the AGM of the International Feltmakers Association, given by May Jacobsen-Hvistendahl, that I began to formulate my own creatures. Gradually they developed their identities, starting with the very elegant creatures that May had shown us and moving on to the strange animals that I am hatching now. I love the way they develop as I make them and how a creature's character appears only when the eyes are placed in position.

I traveled back from the course on the London Underground with my felt carpet, still wet, in a big plastic bag. I wondered why the other passengers were giving me strange looks and then realized that I had created a big puddle. What must they have thought?

Since that time I have worked my way through mountains of wool. I teach felt-making to people of all ages and genders. My school workshops are enjoyed by the children and teachers in equal measure, all of them marveling at the magic of felt. I have even taught felt-making to groups of men who, after initial suspicion, are convinced enough to take wool home with them to play with. They may tell me that it is for their children, but I know better.

Since making those first pieces at the Victoria and Albert Museum, I have produced all sorts of different items in felt. It was after attending a

The projects shown in this book are only the beginning, because you can change an animal's character by altering the color scheme, the animal's shape, or its expression. You can also add items of clothing or decorations, such as felt flowers. All these items can be made from flat felt pieces and sewn onto the finished animal. Experiment and I hope you enjoy making felt creatures as much as I do.

SUE PEARL

Getting Started

Materials and Equipment

The materials used to make felt are very important. Making felt should be a joy, not a chore, so the wool I use is merino, which felts very easily. It is a very fine fiber and, although more expensive than other wool fibers, it felts more quickly than the wool from other breeds of sheep. Merino also takes dyes well and gives a tremendous depth of color. The way the fine fibers mingle also creates excellent color blends, a factor that adds an extra dimension to the appearance of the felt. I use merino in the form of roving (or tops), which is how most wool suppliers sell it. This means the wool has been washed and carded and all the fibers are lying in the same direction.

Merino is also used in the manufacture of needlepunch felt sheets. This felt comes in three weights: 4 oz/100 g, 8 oz/200 g, and 1 lb/400 g. I use the middle weight, as it holds together well and is not too thick. Needlepunch felt is made on a metal bed on which there are rows of small needles that catch the fibers of the wool as it passes over them. The needles go up and down, knitting the fibers together to make a fabric that can be used as it is or wet-felted.

The wool I use for the inner layers of my creatures is from Cheviot sheep. These sheep were found on the hills between England and Scotland (an area known as the Border country), as far back as the fourteenth century but are now bred in Australia, New Zealand, and North America, as well as in the British Isles. Cheviot sheep produce a dense wool fiber that is springy to the touch. Cheviot wool does not felt as quickly and as easily as merino, but when it has felted it is firm and solid — and perfect as a filler. I use it to wrap the animals' basic skeletons before adding color.

Wool fibers are covered in scales which open up when an alkali — that is to say, soap — is used. The opened scales, like hooks, lock on to their neighbors as the fibers are manipulated. The more you rub and tease the fibers, the stronger that bond becomes. In essence you are shrinking the wool — exactly what you would not want to do to a favorite wool sweater.

Soap solution

You should always use pure soapflakes or olive oil soap for the felting process. The felting moment is quite critical and there should be the correct amount of soap: too much and it will not felt, as the fibers will slide around; too little and you will find it difficult to get the fibers to mesh together. It is hard to be precise about the quantity of soap required, because it depends on

Merino wool in jewellike colors is perfect for making felt creatures. White roving forms the body shapes.

Use pure soap flakes or grated olive oil soap to create the soapy solution with which to wet felt the animals.

The skeletons

All the 3-D creatures made in this book are created around a skeleton formed from wire and 1 ft/30 cm long pipe cleaners. I have used copper wire for the projects in this book, but you can use any wire that is sturdy enough to allow the animals to stand. Examples of suitable wire include semi-hard brass, stainless steel, or aluminum. The thickness to use is 17 gauge (0.53 American wire gauge and 0.56 in. SWG or, standard wire gauge). Other materials you will need for most of the animals are beads for eyes. I use 4mm or 5mm black glass beads, which I first pin and then stitch in place with a strong black cotton thread.

To bend the wire to form the skeletons, you will need a pair of flat-nosed pliers; to cut the wire and pipe cleaners you will need a pair of wire cutters.

Preparing the fibers

You will need a pair of wool carders to prepare the merino fibers for felting before the fibers are wrapped around the animals. Carders are wooden paddles that have a cloth of metal hooks stapled on to one side of each paddle. Spinners use carders to comb wool fibers from a sheep's fleece in one direction before they

how hard your water is. As a general guide, the water should feel slightly "soapy." I would recommend adding 1 tablespoon of soap flakes or grated olive oil soap to a medium-sized bowl of water heated to about 55°C or 60°C. (The hotter the water, the faster the fibers will felt.)

If you use artificial detergents, such as a dishwashing (washing-up) liquid, too much foam will be produced. If you use beauty soap, it may have a moisturizer added, which will inhibit the felting process. I prefer to use soap flakes, but olive oil soap is also very good and is easily available.

start to spin. Spinners make rolags — sausage shapes — from the fleece to make the fibers more manageable. In this book, carders are used to bring air into the wool and to separate the fibers so that they cover smoothly and without clumping. If you wish, you can use dog brushes, which are similar to carders but smaller.

The upholstery foam that I use to make needlefelt for decorations is denser than some other types of foam. It is easy to find, as many furniture upholsterers use it and are usually willing to sell small remnants. For most of the

You'll need wire cutters and flat-nosed pliers to create skeletons. Choose tools in sizes that feel most comfortable to handle.

To build a skeleton you will need pipe cleaners, and occasionally copper wire and string. Beads in two sizes are used to make eyes for the animals. Choose the size that best suits your creature.

Wool carders (right) or dog brushes are essential for preparing wool fibers. You'll need a block of upholstery foam and felting needles or punches to make needlefelt.

projects, you will need a piece measuring 4 in./ 10 cm square and 3 in./8 cm thick.

Felting needles have become very popular in recent times; there is a growing band of needle-felters who make wonderful dolls, trolls, and other beasts, as well as jewelry, all without the aid of soap and water. I use felting needles to encourage the wool fibers to bed down in hard-to-reach places and to make sure that the coverage of the piece I am making is complete

before I wet-felt. I suggest that 36 gauge and 38 gauge (36mm and 38mm) felting needles are the best size for the projects in this book.

There is now a needlefelting machine, called an embellisher, which acts and looks like a sewing machine, but uses five or six felting needles instead of a sewing needle. There are different brands and models; the one I use is called Easyneedle. A needlefelting machine has many uses but it is of limited use for this book. However, it is an interesting piece of equipment, and with a little practice you can make all kinds of needlefelt embellishments, such as flowers, for your critters or to decorate a bag.

Basic equipment for wet felting

For wet felting, you will need a medium-sized plastic bowl, a plastic dishwashing (washing-up) brush, a plastic tea tray, and a supply of plastic bubblewrap, which should be cut to a size approximately 6 in./15 cm bigger all round than the tray, unless otherwise specified. When the bubblewrap is placed directly on the work surface or a bamboo mat, the bubblewrap should be about 4 in./10 cm bigger all around than the flat felt piece you intend to make so there is room for the fibers to expand when soapy water is added to the fibers. You may also wish to use tongs to handle the felt when rinsing with very hot water.

If the instructions tell you to finish felting a creature by spinning it in a washing machine, first put it inside the kind of laundry mesh bag used when washing delicate items, such as lingerie. You'll need a bamboo mat when rolling wet felt. Depending on the size of the felt you are making, this might be a small mat of the kind used when preparing sushi, a large reed mat or an old bamboo window blind. When working with pre-felts, you'll need a pair of good quality fabric scissors, along with a tape measure and sewing needles.

Basic wet-felting equipment is easily assembled from around the home.

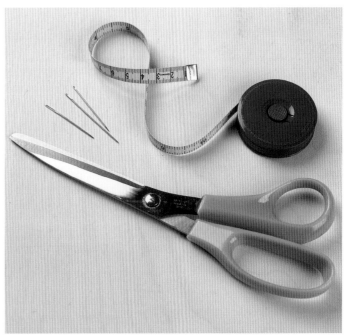

Fabric scissors, a tape measure, and a selection of sewing needles are useful when working with pre-felts.

How to Make Flat Felt

Changing fluffy wool fibers into a compact, dense fabric without any weaving or sewing has always seemed to me to be a magical process. Laying the wool fibers in the correct way so that the fibers shrink and lock together is perhaps the most important element to making the felted animals in this book. The layers of wool must be fluffy and more layers of light, open fibers are preferable to fewer layers of densely packed fibers. If you find it difficult to pull the fibers finely enough in Step 1, use wool carders or dog brushes to brush them open.

The example of flat felt shown here is a two-color sample, but the technique is the same for a piece made from a single color.

TOOLS AND MATERIALS

▶ **2 pieces of bubblewrap, 2 ft/61 cm square**

▶ **1 ½ oz/40 g merino roving in 2 colors**

▶ **Hot, soapy solution**

▶ **Plastic bowl**

▶ **Dishwashing brush**

▶ **Bamboo mat**

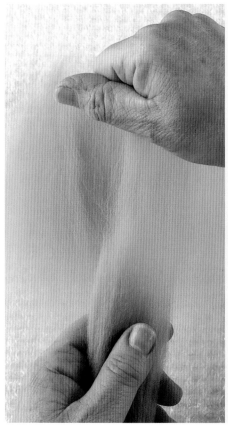

1 Place a sheet of bubblewrap on the work surface, bubble side up. The bubblewrap should be about 4 in./10 cm bigger all around than the flat felt piece you intend to make so there is room for the fibers to expand when water is added. Grasp a bundle of merino roving loosely in one hand. With your fingertips against the base of the thumb of your other hand, pull away fibers from the roving. Lay the fibers in a thin layer on the bubblewrap. Make sure the layer is even and just thick enough to obscure the bubblewrap.

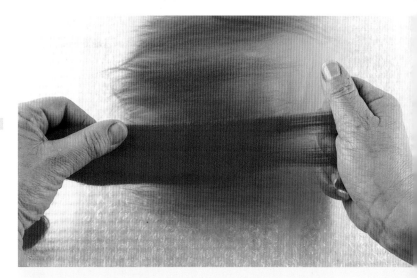

2 Repeat Step 1 with the second color, laying the fibers at right angles to the first layer. Lay enough of the second color to completely cover the first layer. Repeat Step 1 with the first color, laying the fibers at right angles to the fibers in the previous layer.

3 Using a dishwashing brush, shake some of the hot, soapy solution over the square of fibers.

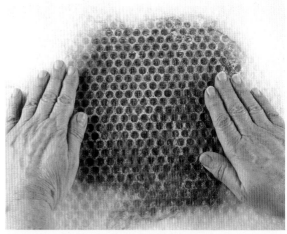

4 Lay the second piece of bubblewrap on top of the wet fibers, bubble side down. Shake a small amount of soapy solution onto the bubblewrap to allow your hands to slide easily across the surface. With your hands flat on the bubblewrap press the soap solution trapped inside the two pieces of bubblewrap to all parts of the wool square without rubbing the plastic layers too much.

5 When the fibers begin to shrink and to adhere to each other, remove the top layer of bubblewrap. Gather the fibers together in a ball and rub the ball on the bottom layer of bubblewrap to encourage the felting process.

6 Lay the bamboo mat on the bubblewrap. Place the felt square on the bamboo mat and roll it backward and forward. The felt will shrink in the direction in which you are rolling. To ensure that the felt will shrink evenly, keep turning the felt one turn to the right. The felt square will eventually shrink by 30 to 35 percent overall.

7 Pick up the felt piece and throw it firmly onto the bamboo mat. Repeat this ten times to shock the wool into shrinking and firming.

How to Make Pre-felt

Pre-felt is a term that covers both wet felt and needlefelt, which is also known as needlefelt. The process for making pre-felt is the same as for making wet felt (see page 16), but pre-felt is not fully felted. Pieces of pre-felt can be cut up and used to create detailed designs with defined outline.

Pre-felt using the two-layer method shown here can be used both wet and dry while needlefelt (see How to Make Needlefelt on page 20) is used dry. After pre-felt details have been added to your project, the whole piece should be wet felted as described in the individual project instructions.

1 Lay a bamboo mat on a flat surface and place a piece of bubblewrap on it, bubble side up. The bubblewrap should be about 4 in./10 cm bigger all around than the flat felt piece you intend to make so there is room for the fibers to expand when water is added. Pull out the merino fibers following the method described in Step 1 on page 16. Lay the fibers on the bubblewrap in one direction to make a square of layered fibers. Make the layer thick enough to obscure the bubbles on the bubblewrap.

2 Repeating Step 1, lay more fibers from the roving at right angles to the first layer of fibers. Make this second layer thick enough to cover the fibers on the first layer.

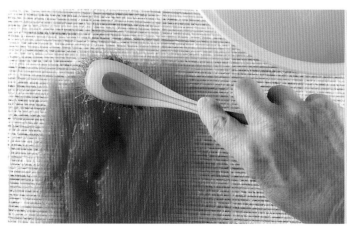

3 Using a dishwashing brush, shake some of the hot, soapy solution over the square of fibers. Apply just enough soapy solution to the square to allow the wool to absorb the water, but not so much that it soaks the fibers.

4 Place a second piece of bubblewrap over the fiber square, bubble side down and sprinkle a little of the soapy solution on the surface of the bubblewrap.

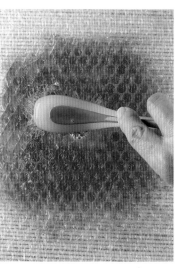

5 With your hands flat on the bubblewrap, press the soapy solution trapped between the two pieces of bubblewrap to all parts of the wool square without rubbing the plastic layers too much. The soapy solution on the top of the bubblewrap will allow your hands to slide easily over the surface.

6 Lift the top layer of bubblewrap to check that all the wool has "wetted" out. This means that the water has all been absorbed by the wool and there are no dry and fluffy patches. If you see any areas that appear dry, shake a little more soapy solution over them, replace the bubblewrap and repeat Step 5.

7 Lift the top layer of bubblewrap and move this to one side. Lift the pre-felt from the bottom sheet of bubblewrap. This is now ready for use in the projects. Pre-felt can also be left to dry and used later.

How to Make Needlefelt

Needlefelt (or needlepunch felt) is made and used dry as a pre-felt, unlike the two-layer method on page 18, which can be used both wet and dry. The difference between the two methods of pre-felt is that needlefelt is usually thick and dense in appearance. Two-layer pre-felt is finer and can be used to build up a background pattern of cut and defined shapes. Needlefelt is created by punching the fibers up and down to knit them together and produces a nonwoven fabric. I have used pre-felt and needlefelt to make flowers, letters, and decorations for the birds and animals before wet felting the pieces as described in the individual instructions.

TOOLS AND MATERIALS

- ▶ 1 ¼ oz/30 g merino roving in one color
- ▶ Pair of wool carders or dog brushes
- ▶ Piece of upholstery foam
- ▶ Felting needle, or felting tool with three needles

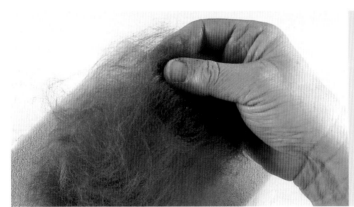

1 Prepare the fibers by carding or brushing them. Lay the fibers in three layers on the foam block. Make sure that the direction of the fibers in each layer is at right angles to those in the layer below.

2 Use the needlefelting needle or tool to punch the carded fibers all over so that they become well integrated. Fold in the wispy edges, and continue to needlefelt to produce a neat shape.

3 Remove the needlefelt piece from the foam block. Turn it over and needlefelt on the other side until the fibers bond together thoroughly.

How to Prepare Needlepunch Felt

Commercial needlepunch felt is made by passing merino fibers over a flat bed with felting needles or hooks which rise and fall to catch the fibers and matt them into a nonwoven fabric. I use needlepunch felt to wrap the animal skeletons prior to wrapping them with colored merino fibers. Needlepunch felt helps smooth out the profile of the animal and provides a good sub-surface onto which the top layer can bond.

TOOLS AND MATERIALS

▶ **I sheet of 8 oz/200 g needlepunch felt**

▶ **Fabric scissors**

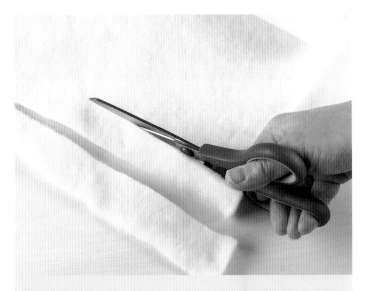

I Lay a sheet of merino needlepunch felt on the work surface. Cut 1 in./2.5 cm strips all the way along the felt, stopping ½ in./12 mm short of the top edge to form a fringe.

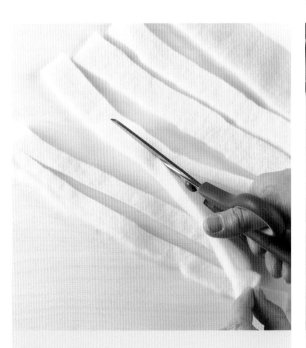

2 Turn the piece so that the uncut edge is in front of you. This time cut along the center of the ¾ in./1.5 cm strips and up to ½ in./12 mm from the top edge, as before.

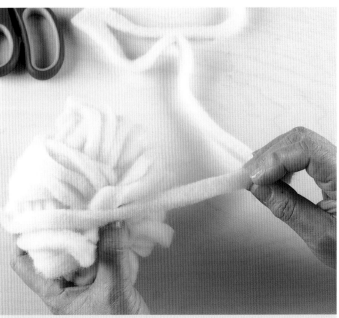

3 This method creates a continuous strip of needlepunch felt. Roll it into a ball, ready for use wrapping skeletons.

How to Make Beads and Buttons

Use this process to create colorful felt beads that can be used as decorative features for the animals. Alternatively, thread these beads onto fine elastic, interspersed with shiny glass beads, to make lovely bracelets, or stick them onto a card base to use as a button or fastening.

TOOLS AND MATERIALS

▶ **1 piece of bubblewrap, 8 in./20 cm square**

▶ **1½ oz/40 g merino roving in four bright colors**

▶ **Hot, soapy solution**

▶ **Plastic bowl**

▶ **Bamboo mat**

▶ **Scissors**

1 Place a sheet of bubblewrap on the work surface, bubble side up. Lay out a layer of fibers no larger than 4 in./10 cm square following the method described in Step 1 on page 16.

2 Lay on the other three colors, making each layer thicker and denser than when preparing ordinary flat felt. Lay each of the four colors at right angles to the layer immediately beneath it.

3 Using your fingers, drop a little of the hot, soapy solution onto the front section of the fiber square.

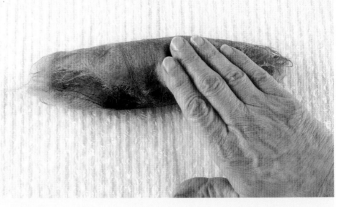

4 Beginning with the edge of the square nearest to you, roll the square tightly into a sausage shape. If the roll feels too dry, sprinkle it with a little more soapy water.

5 Roll the sausage shape backward and forward over the bubblewrap. Keep rolling until you feel the wool shrinking as the fibers begin to felt.

6 Place the sausage shape on the bamboo mat and continue to roll the fibers. This will continue the felting process and the roll will shrink until it is as hard as a pencil. Make the ends pointed as you roll.

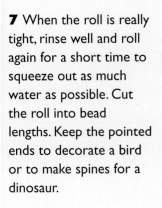

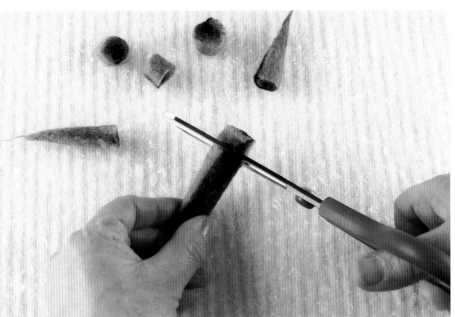

7 When the roll is really tight, rinse well and roll again for a short time to squeeze out as much water as possible. Cut the roll into bead lengths. Keep the pointed ends to decorate a bird or to make spines for a dinosaur.

The Projects

Alphabet Panel with Pockets

This project shows how to make a three-dimensional felt piece. Making the pockets can be a starting point for progressing to more complicated seamless projects, such as bags, or hats. This project makes use of pre-felts for the letters. You may like to use the same technique to make a name to stitch onto a child's coat.

TOOLS AND MATERIALS

- ▶ **2 pieces of bubblewrap, 3 ft/91 cm x 2 ft/61 cm**
- ▶ **Bamboo mat**
- ▶ **Merino roving: 3 oz/80 g in white and 2 oz/50 g in blue-green**
- ▶ **Fabric scissors**
- ▶ **Heavy-duty plastic bag**
- ▶ **Colored letters, cut from pre-felt (see How to Make Pre-felt, page 18)**
- ▶ **Hot, soapy solution**
- ▶ **Plastic bowl**
- ▶ **Dishwashing brush**
- ▶ **UNFELTED SIZE: 12 in./30 cm x 10 in./26 cm**
- ▶ **FINISHED SIZE: 9 in./23 cm x 8 in./20 cm**

Suspend the alphabet panel with tabs sewn on the back, or use a dowel to attach it to a wall.

I Place a sheet of bubblewrap, bubble side up, on the bamboo mat. Lay three layers of white fibers at right angles to each other, as shown in Step 1 on page 16. Cut out three rectangles from the plastic bag, each rectangle 2¾ in./7 cm x 2¼ in./5.5 cm to form resists for the pockets. These resists will prevent the fibers of the pocket felting into the fibers of the panel and will create the pocket opening. Position the plastic resists on the fibers.

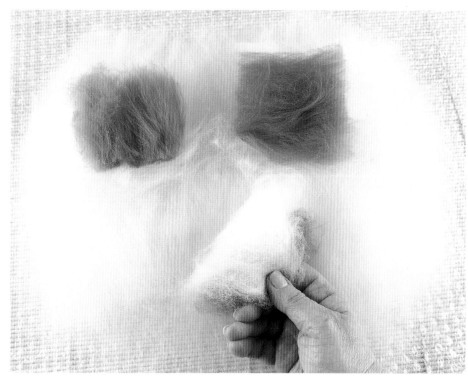

2 Pull out two layers of white fiber and one layer in a color of your choice to make rectangles to lay over the plastic resists. Make sure that the fibers overlap the sides and bottom edge of the plastic resists by ½ in./1.5 cm so the pockets will be well attached on three sides.

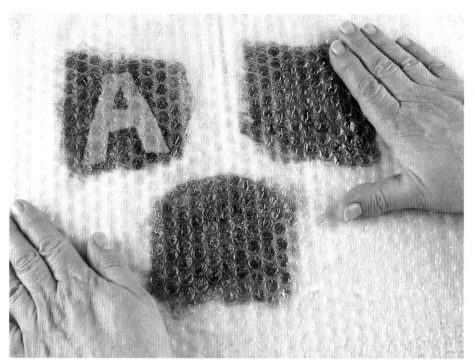

3 Place the pre-felt letters onto the background color patches. Sprinkle the whole piece with hot, soapy solution and place the second sheet of bubblewrap on top, bubble side down. Pour a little soapy water over the smooth side of the bubblewrap and begin to felt the panel as described in Steps 3 and 4 on page 17.

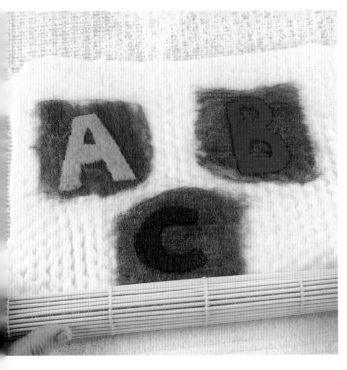

4 When the wool fibers begin to felt, roll the felt piece in the bamboo mat. To ensure that the felt will shrink evenly, keep turning the felt one turn to the right .

5 As the felt shrinks, the plastic resists will begin to poke out from the pockets. Remove the plastic and continue rolling the felt in the bamboo mat.

6 Put your hand inside a pocket and rub hard along the top edge, to harden it. Repeat with the other pockets. Roll the whole piece a few more times inside the bamboo mat. Throw the panel repeatedly onto the bamboo mat for about two minutes to increase the shrinkage. Rinse well and leave to dry.

Fancy Fish

This simple fish can be finished with decorative scales cut from needlefelt and needled onto the wrapped fish before the felting process. A school of these fish would look good hanging in the corner of a room.

TOOLS AND MATERIALS

- Ten 1 ft/30 cm pipe cleaners

- 1 ft/30 cm copper wire

- Wire cutters

- Flat-nosed pliers

- Undyed merino needlepunch felt, 15 in./38 cm square, cut into ½ in./12 mm strips

- 1½ oz/30 g white cheviot roving

- Pair of wool carders or dog brushes

- Merino roving: ⅓ oz/10 g rose, ¾ oz/20 g medium green, 2 oz/50 g cornflower

- Flat felt in ⅓ oz/10 g each green and lime green (see How to Make Flat Felt on page 16)

- Fabric scissors

- Felting needle

- Shallow tray

- 1 piece of bubblewrap, large enough to line the tray

- Hot, soapy solution

- Plastic bowl

- Dishwashing brush

- Mesh laundry bag

- 2 black glass beads

- Needle and yellow and black thread

- FINISHED SIZE:
  8½ in./22 cm x
  10 in./25.5 cm

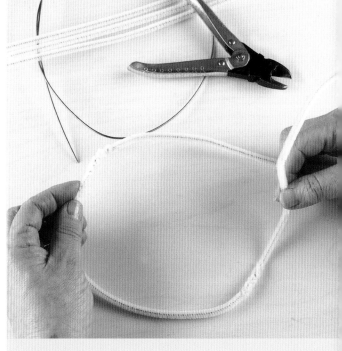

1 Join two pipe cleaners together to make a long piece. Cut a piece of copper wire the same length as the joined pipe cleaners. Repeat to make a second long piece and twist these two pieces together.

2 Wrap the extra-long pipe cleaner around the copper wire, and bend it into a circle. Cut off any excess wire, making sure you leave pipe cleaner "tails" free of wire. Complete the circle by wrapping the ends of the pipe cleaners around each other. Bend another pipe cleaner into a smaller circle to form the fish's tail.

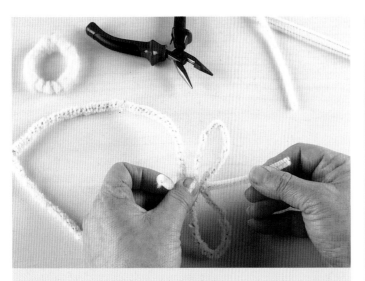
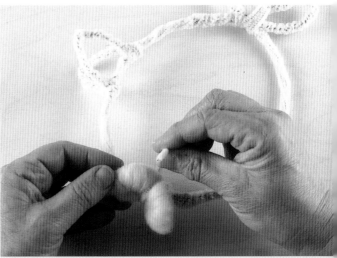

3 Place the large circle on a flat surface with the joined section to the left. To make a tail for the fish, squeeze the smaller circle flat to make an elongated loop. Cut a pipe cleaner in half and use this to fix the tail to the right-hand side of the large circle. To form a mouth, bend one pipe cleaner around twice to make a small circle.

4 Wrap the mouth with slivers of cheviot roving then fix it to the body using half a pipe cleaner. Cut another pipe cleaner in half and make two fins; fix these to what will be the bottom edge of the body. Stuff the skeleton with loose cheviot roving, making sure that the wool spills out of the open sides. When you are happy with the shape of the fish, wrap the body with needlepunch felt.

Add color and felt the fish

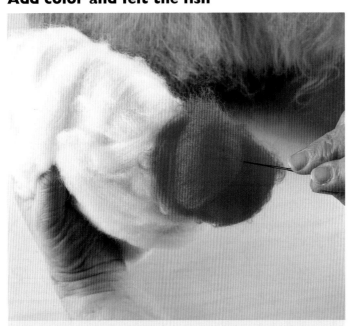

5 Card or brush the merino fibers. Use rose fibers to wrap the mouth, fixing the fibers in place with a felting needle.

6 Wrap the fins and the tail with mid-green merino fibers.

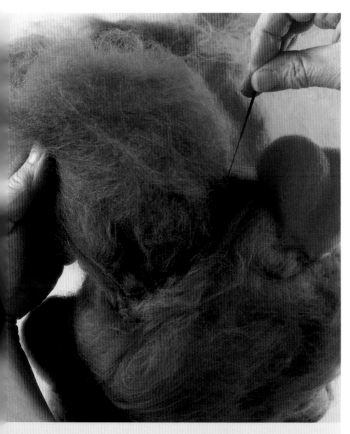

8 Cut the green flat felt fin to shape. Cut out two gills from the piece of lime-green flat felt and stitch them in place with a needle and yellow thread.

7 Wrap the body with cornflower-colored fibers, making sure that there is no white showing. To make a top fin, make a square from three layers of mid-green fibers. Ensure each layer crosses the other at right angles. Place this square at the top of the fish. Lay another layer of mid-green fibers each side of the body, overhanging the top of the fish by 1 in./2.5 cm. These extra layers must run perpendicular to the layers below. Lay some more cornflower in the opposite direction, to make sure that the top fin will be well bonded to the body when it is wet felted. Use a felting needle to fix the fin fibers into the body.

To wet felt the fish, line the tray with bubblewrap, bubble side up. Make a soapy solution and use the dishwashing brush to shake hot, soapy solution over the fibers. The hotter the water, the more quickly the wool will felt. Gently rub the fish to felt it.

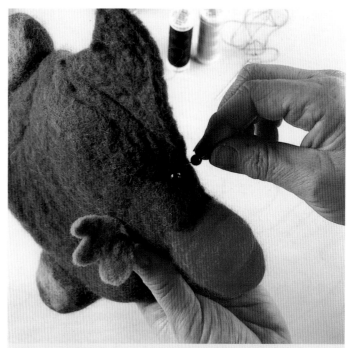

9 Stitch the eyes in place with a needle and black thread.

Shaker Snake

Far from being scary, this brightly colored rattlesnake is guaranteed to cheer anybody up on the gloomiest of days! Snakes, of course, come in many colors and patterns so you can create some wondrous reptiles. As an alternative to this snake, make a draft stopper (draught excluder) by stuffing one leg of a pair of pantyhose with cheviot roving, then wrapping the whole leg with slivers of roving. Finish off the snake with strips of needlepunch felt in assorted colors.

TOOLS AND MATERIALS

▶ Approximately twelve 1 ft/30 cm pipe cleaners

▶ 2 ft/61 cm copper wire

▶ Wire cutters

▶ Flat-nosed pliers

▶ 1¼ oz/30 g white cheviot roving

▶ Undyed merino needlepunch felt, 20 in./51 cm square, cut into ½ in./12 mm strips

▶ Pair of wool carders or dog brushes

▶ Merino roving: 3½ oz/100 g bright yellow, sliver of scarlet

▶ Needlefelt in ⅓ oz/10 g each of vibrant lilac, lime green, and blue-violet; small handful black (see How to Make Needlefelt on page 20)

▶ Fabric scissors

▶ Felting needle

▶ Shallow tray

▶ 1 piece of bubblewrap, large enough to line the tray

▶ Hot, soapy solution

▶ Plastic bowl

▶ Dishwashing brush

▶ Mesh laundry bag

▶ 2 black glass beads

▶ FINISHED SIZE: 20 in./51 cm long

1 Join three pipe cleaners to make an extra-long length. Repeat this twice so you end up with three extra-long pipe cleaners. Twist these three long pipe cleaners together around the copper wire.

2 To create the snake's head, bend back the wire and pipe cleaner length to make a loop about 6 in./15 cm long at one end. Twist the loose ends down to hold the loop in place. Wrap the whole piece with three more regular pipe cleaners as shown.

3 Stuff some loose cheviot roving inside the head cavity, then wrap the head and body in slivers of cheviot roving.

4 Continue wrapping until the body is between 2½–3 in./6–7.5 cm thick, then completely cover with strips of needlepunch felt.

Add color and felt the snake

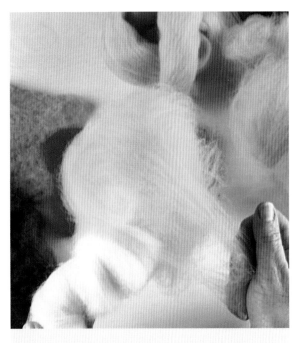

5 Card or brush the fibers. Start to wrap the head with bright yellow fibers, making sure you cross the fibers across each other as you wrap.

6 When the body and head of the snake are completely covered, cut circles from the needlefelt. Fix these in groups around the body of the snake with the felting needle. Wet felt the snake following Steps 8–11 of Groovy Cat on pages 62–63.

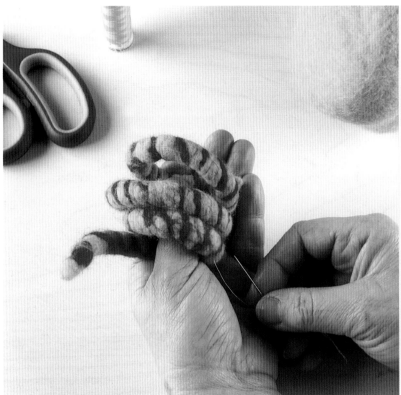

7 To create the snake's rattle, make a long felted sausage from the bright yellow fibers. To do this, wet your hands with a small amount of hot soapy solution and roll a length of fiber between them. Before the sausage is fully felted, wrap a sliver of scarlet merino fiber around the sausage. Finish felting, rinse well, and leave to dry. Bend the sausage shape into a spiral and use a needle and thread to hold the spiral in position.

8 Fit the sewn rattle onto the end of the snake and sew in place with a needle and yellow thread.

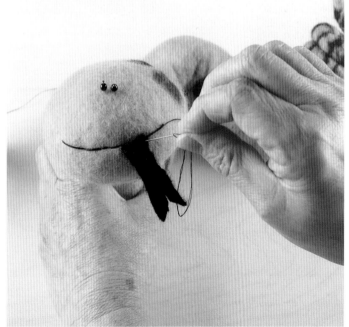

9 Cut out a forked tongue from the black needlefelt. Using black thread, stitch a mouth across the top end of the head, then stitch the tongue in place. Stitch the eyes in position.

Simple Felt Picture

This project is made from flat felt, which is the basis for all felt panels or pictures. It is important to make a good foundation of three or more layers to support the decorative elements. Here, the piece is decorated with flower and leaf motifs cut from pre-felt and needlefelt. Follow the instructions for How to Make Pre-felt on page 18 and How to Make Needlefelt on page 20 for the methods. You can also add scraps of silk or cotton to the surface of the picture, then lay an extremely fine layer of wool fibers over the scraps to integrate them into the picture. The wool fibers will shrink and hold the silk or cotton in place.

TOOLS AND MATERIALS

▷ **Merino roving: 3 oz/80 g in white and 2 oz/50 g in assorted colors**

▷ **Bamboo mat**

▷ **2 pieces of bubblewrap, 3 ft/91 cm x 2 ft/61 cm**

▷ **1½ oz/40 g of pre-felt in assorted colors**

▷ **¾ oz/20 g of needlefelt in assorted colors**

▷ **Fabric scissors**

▷ **Hot, soapy solution**

▷ **Plastic bowl**

▷ **Dishwashing brush**

▷ **UNFELTED SIZE: 15 in./38 x 12 in./30 cm**

▷ **FINISHED SIZE: 12½ in./32 cm x 9 in./23 cm**

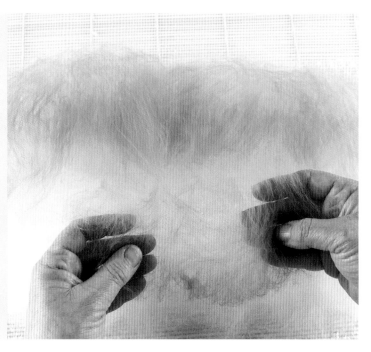

1 Place a sheet of bubblewrap on the work surface, bubble side up. Lay three layers of white fibers at right angles to each other, as shown on page 16. Add a fourth layer in one color or use a number of different shades to form a mottled effect. This will form the background of your picture. Make sure the fibers in the fourth layer are laid at right angles to those in the third layer.

This charming felt picture was inspired by a child's drawing. In fact, the project is ideal for youngsters to make with a little adult assistance.

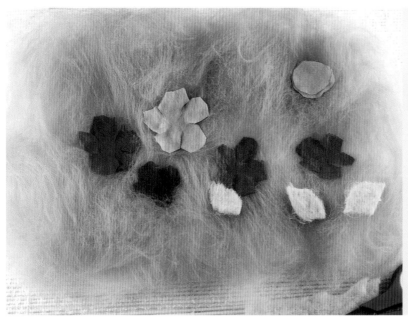

2 Make some pre-felt for the flowers and needlefelt for the leaves following the instructions on pages 18 and 20. Pre-felt will give a delicate appearance to the flowers, and needlefelt will lend the leaves a solid effect. Arrange the flower and leaf shapes on the background fibers.

3 Keep the design to the center of the panel as the edge will be thinner and less able to support the motifs. Motifs can be overlapped but try not to overcrowd the design: when the wool felts, the spaces in between the motifs will be reduced and some of the finer details may be lost.

4 Sprinkle the wool surface with soapy solution and place the second sheet of bubblewrap on top, bubble side down. Wet felt the piece following Step 4 on page 17. When the wool begins to shrink, follow Steps 5–7. Rinse well and leave to dry.

In this section you'll find instructions for making a flock of multicolored birds and a rather charming duck.

Two-legged Creatures

Basic Bird Skeleton

Follow the steps for the skeleton on pages 44–46 to make the basic form for a kooky standing bird or a bendy-legged bird that will sit on a shelf or desktop. On page 49, you'll find instructions for making a duck, which is a variation on the basic bird skeleton.

The colorful details to the birds' bodies are made from needlefelt, for which you will find ingredients and instructions on page 20, How to Make Needlefelt.

TOOLS AND MATERIALS

▶ **Approximately ten 1 ft/30 cm pipe cleaners**

▶ **1 ft/30 cm copper wire**

▶ **Wire cutters**

▶ **Flat-nosed pliers**

▶ **1¼ oz/30 g white cheviot roving**

▶ **Undyed merino needlepunch felt, 2 ft/61 cm square, cut into ½ in./12 mm strips**

▶ **Ball of thin linen string**

▶ **Fabric scissors**

▶ **Tape measure**

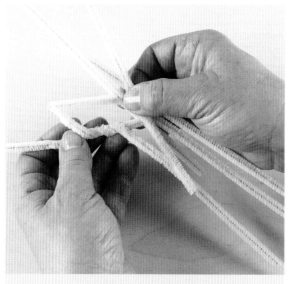 

1 Take six pipe cleaners and separate into two groups of three. Overlap one end of each group by the ends of the other group by 3 in./7.5 cm. Twist these overlapped ends together to make three double-length pipe cleaners. Each piece will be the same length.

2 Loop one end of the bundle of pipe cleaners to make three toes by folding back 5½ in./14 cm from the end and twisting the loose ends tight into the pipe cleaners. Repeat at the other end of the bundle so you have six toes.

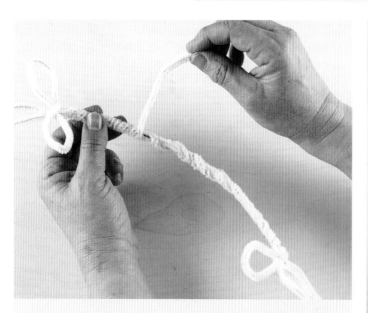 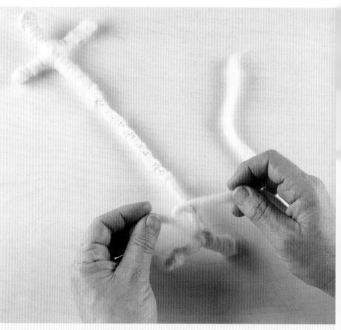

3 Wrap the bundle of pipe cleaners around the length of copper wire. Overlap the wire with extra pipe cleaners to smooth and strengthen it. (If you want to make a bird with bendy legs, omit the copper wire from this step.)

4 Use strips of needlepunch felt to wrap the feet, then continue to wrap all the way up the leg. Make sure the needlepunch felt completely covers the pipe cleaners.

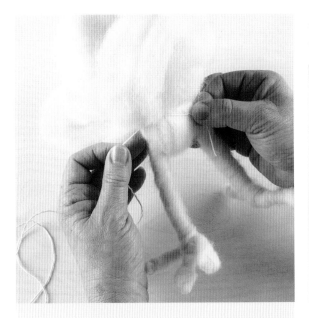

5 Bend the leg piece in half so that the feet line up. Take 30 in./76 cm of cheviot roving folded into thirds. Hook this bundle over the bend in the legs to form the body. Tie string tightly around the roving to make a waist.

6 Bend a pipe cleaner into a double circle, and leave the ends free. Bend half a pipe cleaner in half to make a beak. Twist the legs of this pipe cleaner together leaving the ends free. Wrap the free ends over the circle to hold everything in place.

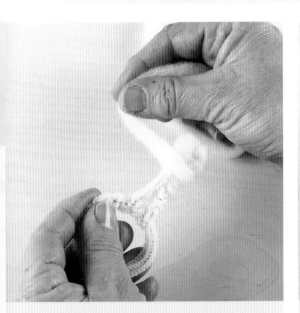

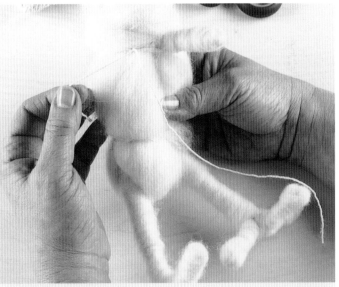

7 Fix the loop onto the circle and wrap the tails over to hold it in place. Squeeze the loop together to make an elongated beak then wrap it with a sliver of cheviot roving. Wrap the circle in the same way.

8 Tie a length of string tightly around the cheviot roving 1½ in./4 cm from the top of the body (made in Step 5). This is the position for sliding on the beak. Slide the wrapped circle and beak over the top of the head and slip into place over the tied string.

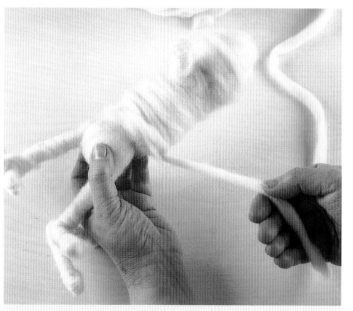

9 Wrap the bird completely with slivers of cheviot roving, bulking it out as desired to make a wide middle or a fat bottom. The wool fibers will shrink by about a third, so don't skimp on wool at this stage or you'll end up with a very skinny bird!

10 Wrap strips of needlepunch felt all over the body (except the beak) and under the torso so that the bird's body looks like an Egyptian mummy. This smoothes out the shape and makes a good foundation for the finishing layers of colored wool fibers.

Exotic Bird

Multicolored birds are some of the most successful creatures that can be made with my felting method. The range of brilliantly colored merino fibers available are ideal for tropical plummage and eye-catching combinations. To make a bendy-legged bird that will sit, omit the copper wire from Step 1 of the Basic Bird Skeleton then add color as normal.

TOOLS AND MATERIALS

▶ **Basic Bird Skeleton from page 44**

▶ **Pair of wool carders or dog brushes**

▶ **Merino roving: ⅓ oz/10 g bright yellow, 1½ oz/30 g blue violet, ¾ oz/20 g bright cherry, ¾ oz/20 g vibrant lilac**

▶ **Needlefelt in 1¼ oz/30 g bright cherry, for the details**

▶ **Felting needle**

▶ **Shallow tray**

▶ **Hot, soapy solution**

▶ **Plastic bowl**

▶ **Dishwashing brush**

▶ **2 black glass beads**

▶ **Needle and black thread**

▶ **FINISHED SIZE: 9 in./23 cm wide with wings spread x 9 in./23 cm high**

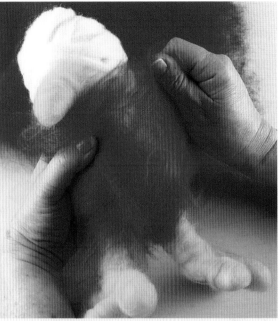

1 Card or brush the merino fibers. Wrap the feet, legs, and beak in yellow merino fibers, making sure that all the strips of white needlepunch felt are covered. Cross the fibers randomly wherever you can, as crossing them will encourage the wool to felt in the wet-felting process.

2 Wrap the body in vibrant lilac fibers. Wrap between the legs, crossing the fibers as you layer the wool. Continue to wrap until the bird is covered in colored fibers.

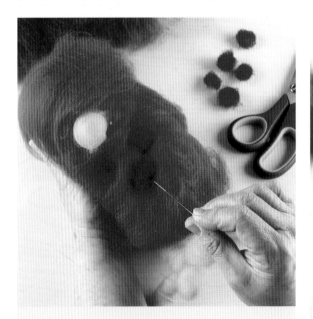

3 Cut small circles from bright cherry needlefelt and fix them in place on the bird's belly, using a felting needle.

4 Lay out the wings and the tail using blue-violet and vibrant lilac merino fibers. Lay the fibers from chest to wing, making sure that you cross the direction of each layer.

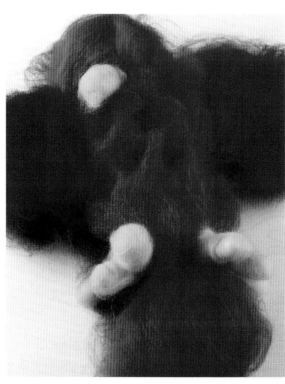

6 On the front of the bird, lay bright cherry fibers in layers from the chest down to the tail feathers.

5 Turn the bird over and lay fibers from the head, over the top of the wings, down its back to the tail feathers.

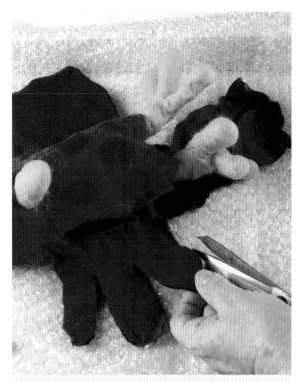

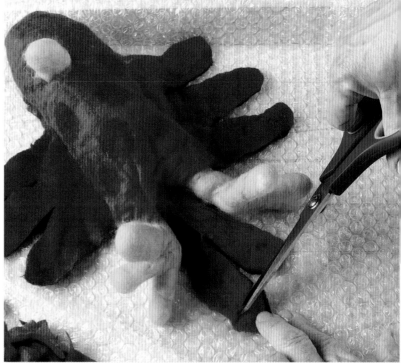

7 Wet felt the bird following Steps 6–8 on page 51. When the bird is becoming well felted, cut the wings to suggest feathers.

8 Cut the tail feathers. Rinse well in very hot, then cold water, then put into a mesh laundry bag and place in a washing machine on a spin cycle. Remove the bird from the bag, and leave to dry naturally. When the bird is dry, pin and stitch the eyes in position.

Village Duck

In the Cotswold village where I live, a brave duck and drake often search my garden for a new location for duckling production. Luckily for them, my cat Zebi is 20 years old, completely deaf, and spends most of her day asleep. She has better things to do than run after ducks. To make Bert, the duck on the left, follow the instructions for the Basic Bird Skeleton on page 44, but change the beak shape, as described on page 50. The duck looks good with a fine set of feathers sewn around its head. Ducks have such wonderful plumage, so mimic Mother Nature's color scheme and create a really fancy water bird.

TOOLS AND MATERIALS

▶ **Prepared Basic Bird body from page 44**

▶ **Two 1 ft/30 cm pipe cleaners**

▶ **Wire cutters**

▶ **Undyed merino needlepunch felt, 2 ft/61 cm square, cut into three ½ in./12 mm strips**

▶ **Pair of wool carders or dog brushes**

▶ **Merino roving: 1¼ oz/30 g lime, ¾ oz/20 g each of bright yellow, citrus green, and mustard**

▶ **Felting needle**

▶ **Shallow tray**

▶ **1 piece of bubblewrap, large enough to line the tray**

▶ **Hot, soapy solution**

▶ **Plastic bowl**

▶ **Dishwashing brush**

▶ **Mesh laundry bag**

▶ **2 black glass beads**

▶ **Needle and thread**

▶ **FINISHED SIZE: 8 in./20.5 cm wide with wings spread x 11 in./28 cm high**

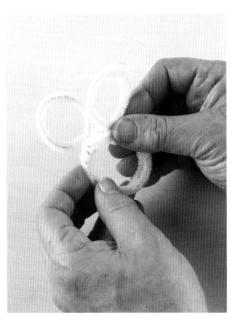

1 Bend one pipe cleaner into a circle, wrapping it twice around itself. Leave two "tails." With the wire cutters, cut a second pipe cleaner in half. Make a loop from each half of the pipe cleaner and fix these to the circle. This will be the beak.

2 Wrap the duck's beak in needlepunch felt, then wrap the circle in the same way. Slide the wrapped circle and beak over the top of the duck's head and slip in place over the tied string as demonstrated in Step 8 of the Basic Bird Skeleton on page 45.

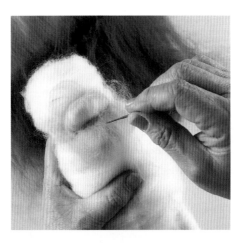

3 Card or brush the dyed merino fibers and leave in separate color piles. Wrap the beak in yellow merino fibers, making sure that all the strips of white needlepunch felt are covered. Use a felting needle to fix the fibers around the beak.

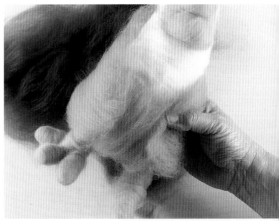

4 Wrap the feet and legs, crossing the fibers randomly wherever you can, as this will encourage the wool to felt in the wet-felting process. Prepare the wings, by laying three layers of fibers is at right angles to each other. Wrap fibers around the body and the legs, like a diaper.

5 Lay fibers over the head and across the chest to the wings. Make sure that the fibers cross each other and lie in different directions. Make the tail feathers by laying fibers from the front of the body and across the wings. Continue to use the felting needle to fix fibers around the beak.

6 Line the tray with bubblewrap, bubble side up. Make a soapy solution and use the dishwashing brush to shake the hot, soapy solution over the duck. The hotter the water, the more quickly the wool will felt. Gently rub the duck to felt it, starting with the feet and beak.

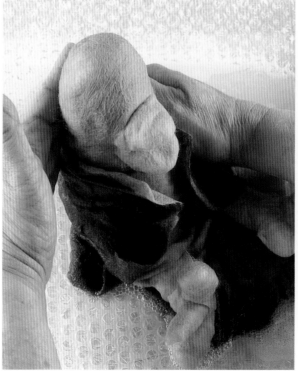

8 Sit the duck upright. Wrap the wings around the back of the body and rub until the fibers are thoroughly shrunk and felted. Rinse well with very hot water followed by very cold water. Place the duck in a mesh laundry bag and put it in the washing machine on a spin cycle. Leave to dry naturally before stitching the eyes in position.

7 Wet felt the chest and the wings by gently rubbing them with your fingers. Massage the head and tail feathers in the same way.

VARIATIONS:
A Flock of
Many Colors

Each bird can easily be customized by adding a pretty flower to the head or giving them a buttonhole decoration or daisy chain necklace.

Make a punky bird by using the pointed ends left over from making felt beads (see How to Make Beads and Buttons on page 22).

Once you have mastered the four-legged skeleton, you can let your imagination run wild and create a whole menagerie of delightful creatures. Here, you'll find ideas for making a cat, dogs and a pig.

Four-legged Creatures

Basic Animal Skeleton

This is the basic skeleton for a critter with four legs and a tail. When you make one of the animals, you will find that each one has its own features in addition to the basic shape. It is these that give the critter its particular look and character.

The basic skeleton is be wrapped slightly differently for each project so that the cat will be slim, the dog will have thicker legs, and the pig will be more solid looking with a fatter body. Get out your pipe cleaners, make a skeleton, then create your animal.

TOOLS AND MATERIALS

▷ **Approximately twenty 1 ft/30 cm pipe cleaners**

▷ **1 ft/30 cm copper wire**

▷ **Wire cutters**

▷ **Flat-nosed pliers**

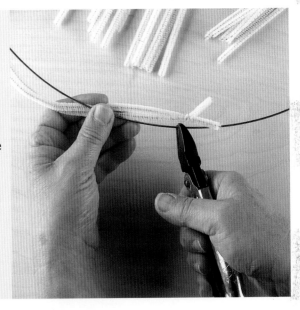

1 Twist two pipe cleaners together, leaving 1½ in./ 4 cm free at both ends. Measure the wire against the twisted length of the pipe cleaners and cut with the wire cutter.

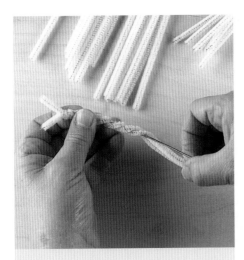

2 Twist the two pipe cleaners over the wire evenly, making sure that the wire is well covered.

3 Cut off the excess wire that extends beyond the twisted part. The piece you have made will make two legs. Put this aside for use in Step 5.

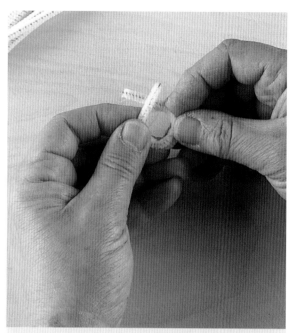

4 Cut two pipe cleaners in half to make four pieces, for paws. Make a circle with one half piece and twist the ends around this circle.

5 Attach the circle to one end of the twisted pipe cleaner legs made in Step 3. Twist the free ends around the circle to hold it firmly in place.

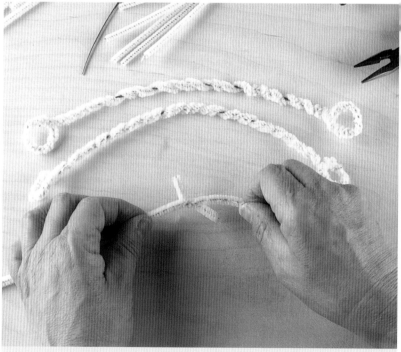

6 Using the flat-nosed pliers, squeeze all the pipe cleaner ends around the circle so that no wire protrudes. Repeat to finish all four paws.

7 To make the animal's back, take two pipe cleaners and twist them together, end to end. Wrap the free ends back on to the pipe cleaners to make a smooth finish.

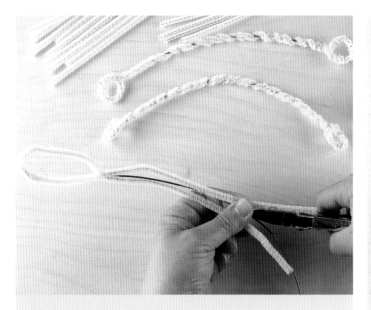

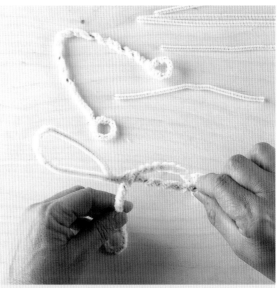

8 Bend this long pipe cleaner in half and twist it to make a tail approximately 3½ in./9 cm long when measured from the joined end. Cut a 4 in./10 cm length of wire to support the body and twist the doubled pipe cleaner over the wire, as in Step 2.

9 Cut a pipe cleaner in half and set aside. Fold a leg piece in half and fit it over the twisted body at the tail end. Fix the legs in place by wrapping and twisting one of the pipe cleaner halves where the legs join the body.

10 Repeat Step 9 to fix the front legs at the other end of the body length, leaving two free pipe cleaner ends.

11 To make the head, take three pipe cleaners and use them to make three circles approximately 2 in./5 cm in diameter. Use one pipe cleaner for each circle.

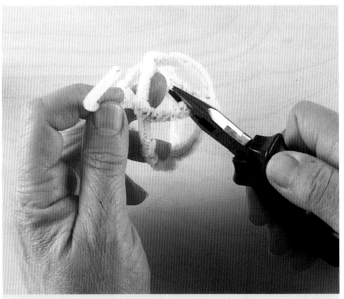

12 Place one circle inside another to make a ball shape. Using a pipe cleaner cut in half, fix the circles in place on both sides by wrapping where the circle join.

13 Place the third circle over the other two to complete the ball shape and wrap all the joints as in Step 12. Use the flat-nosed pliers to squeeze the joints, to make sure there are no wires protruding.

14 Cut a pipe cleaner in half and use the pieces to make an ear on each side of the head, wrapping the ends around one of the circles that form the head.

15 Attach the head to the body with the free pipe cleaner ends. To make sure the head fits firmly, use another pipe cleaner to secure it to the body.

Groovy Cat

Ginsberg, the ginger tom (above right), has a pink felt tongue but no whiskers. By changing details like these, you can give your animals their own individual character.

This cat is made from the Basic Animal Skeleton on pages 55–58. The tail, head, and feet are part of the character of the cat, as cats tend to walk on their toes whereas dogs walk on their feet. The cat's head is rounded and the ears are open and set on either side of the top of the head. Cats often have patchy markings, so Groovy Cat has a purple bib and two striped legs.

The positioning of the eyes gives the cat its personality, so play around with the beads before sewing them on. I find pinning them in place first helps. By shortening the body, leg, and tail length but keeping the head the same size, you could turn this cat into a sweet little kitten.

TOOLS AND MATERIALS

- ▶ **Basic Animal Skeleton from page 55**

- ▶ **Undyed merino needlepunch felt, 2 ft/61 cm square, cut into ½ in./12 mm strips**

- ▶ **¾ oz/20 g white cheviot roving**

- ▶ **Pair of wool carders or wire dog brushes**

- ▶ **Merino roving: 1 ½ oz/30 g each in green and purple**

- ▶ **Needlefelt in ⅓ oz/10 g purple (see How to Make Needlefelt on page 20)**

- ▶ **Fabric scissors**

- ▶ **Felting punch or felting needle**

- ▶ **Shallow tray**

- ▶ **1 piece of bubblewrap, large enough to line the tray**

- ▶ **Hot, soapy solution**

- ▶ **Plastic bowl**

- ▶ **Dishwashing brush**

- ▶ **Mesh laundry bag**

- ▶ **2 black glass beads**

- ▶ **Needle and black thread**

- ▶ **Colorless nylon fishing line**

- ▶ **Finished size: 8 in./20 cm long x 7 in./18 cm high**

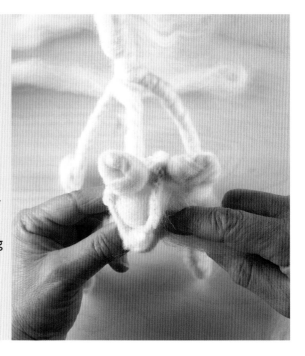

1 Wrap the cat's feet with strips of merino needlepunch felt. Start by winding strips around the circle of the foot, making sure there are no gaps and that the wire skeleton is completely covered.

2 Wrap the ears and tail in the same way, then stuff some cheviot roving into the head cavity, making sure that the wool spills out of the open sides. This wool stuffing will shrink and harden in the felting process.

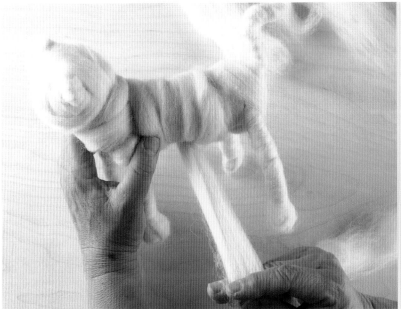

3 Wrap the legs with strips of needlepunch felt. Take a length of cheviot roving and split it lengthways into ½ in./12 mm strips. Use these strips to wrap the whole body so that the wrapping fills out the shape and the cat looks like an Egyptian mummy.

Add color and felt the cat

4 Put the wrapped cat to one side and prepare the green and purple merino fibers for the final wrapping. Using wool carders or dog brushes, brush the fibers out in one direction to make light and fluffy batts.

5 Use a layer of carded purple wool to wrap the feet. Wrap the legs with green wool. Add more layers of green and purple, making sure that none of the white roving is visible. To help the felting process, the fibers should be crossed and wrapped in different directions.

6 Continue to wrap the cat with the green fibers, making sure that features such as the tail and ears are well covered. Make sure that the joints where the legs meet the body are also completely covered. Make stripes around the two front legs with purple fibers.

7 Cut out shapes in purple needlefelt for the bib area under the chin and for other patches on the body. Fix these pieces of needlefelt in place with a felting punch or felting needle. Stab the felting punch through the colored patches into the cat to secure the needlefelt to the body.

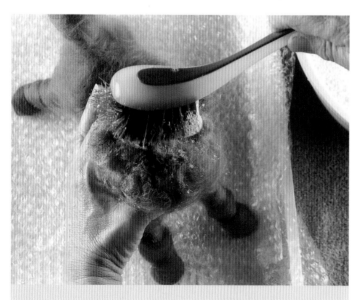

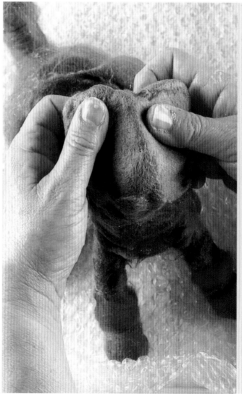

9 Starting at the ears, gently massage the cat to felt the wool. After the ear, move on to the nose and the rest of the head.

8 Line the tray with bubblewrap, bubble side up. Make a hot soapy solution and use the dishwashing brush to shake the soapy solution over the cat. The water should be as hot as possible; the hotter the water, the more quickly the wool will felt.

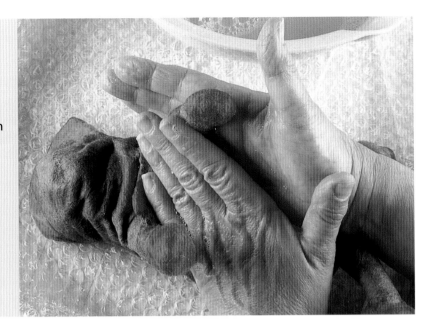

10 Repeat the massaging action for the feet, making sure that the colors stay in the right positions.

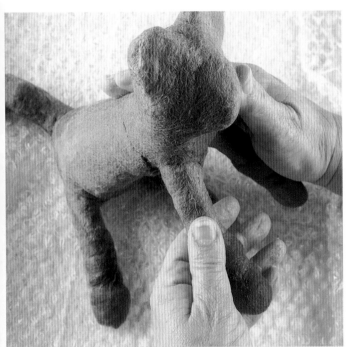

11 Massage the legs, tail, and body with the soapy water. The felting process is improved by constant rubbing and massaging, so mold the cat with your hands to create the desired shape. When you are satisfied, plunge the cat into a bowl of very hot water and then into cold water. Repeat this process to harden the felt. To harden it further, place the cat inside a mesh laundry bag and put it into the washing machine on a spin-only cycle. Alternatively, squeeze it well and leave it to dry.

12 When the cat is dry, sew on the black beads with a needle and black thread. To make a mouth like an upside-down T, take the needle and thread through the head to just below the nose. Use nylon fishing line to make whiskers. Make a knot on one side of the cheek, then pull the nylon through. Make a knot on the other cheek and cut. Repeat twice more, then trim the whiskers to the desired length.

Spotty Dog

This charming Spotty Dog is built around the Basic Animal Skeleton on page 55, just like Groovy Cat. However, there are some differences between the dog and the cat: the dog's feet are flatter, the tail is shorter, and the position of the ears is different. The Spotty Dog is a dalmation, so it is decorated with black spots on a white background. If you have a favorite dog you would like to model, simply change the colors and decorative features.

TOOLS AND MATERIALS

▶ **Basic Animal Skeleton from page 55**

▶ **Approximately five 1 ft/30 cm pipe cleaners**

▶ **Flat-nosed pliers**

▶ **¾ oz/20 g white cheviot roving**

▶ **Undyed merino needlepunch felt, 20 in./51 cm square, cut into ½ in./12 mm strips**

▶ **Pair of wool carders or wire dog brushes**

▶ **Merino roving: 2½ oz/60 g white, ¾ oz/20 g black**

▶ **Needlefelt in ¾ oz/20 g black and ⅓ oz/10 g pink (see How to Make Needlefelt on page 20)**

▶ **Fabric scissors**

▶ **Felting needle**

▶ **Shallow tray**

▶ **1 piece of bubblewrap, large enough to line the tray**

▶ **Hot, soapy solution**

▶ **Plastic bowl**

▶ **Dishwashing brush**

▶ **Mesh laundry bag**

▶ **2 black glass beads**

▶ **Needle and black thread**

▶ **FINISHED SIZE: 8 in./20 cm long x 7 in./18 cm high**

1 Adapt the Basic Animal Skeleton by giving the body a shorter tail. Wrap an additional pipe cleaner around the tail to strengthen and thicken it. Make the head and ears by following Steps 11–14, but make the ears from three-quarters of a pipe cleaner and bend them down.

2 Attach the head to the body with the free pipe cleaner ends. To make sure the head fits firmly, use another pipe cleaner to secure it to the body. If any wires stick up, squeeze them flat with the flat-nosed pliers.

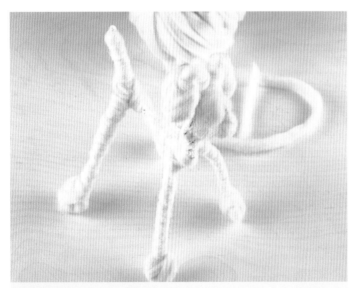

3 Use a quarter of a pipe cleaner to wrap around one of the crossovers of circles to make a nose. Stuff the head cavity with loose cheviot roving, making sure that the wool spills out of the open sides. This wool stuffing will shrink and harden in the felting process. Wrap the nose with a sliver of cheviot roving.

4 Wrap the entire body with strips of needlepunch felt. Wrap the torso, tail, feet, legs, and feet.

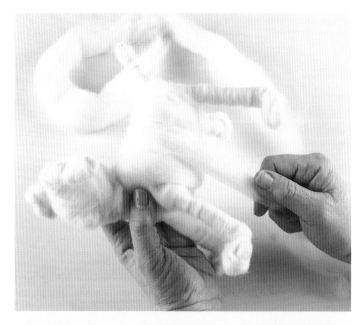

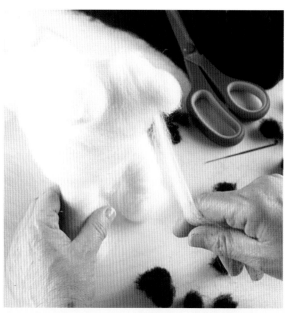

5 Wrap the head and neck with cheviot roving. Build up the body by padding out the dog's belly with some folded cheviot roving. When you are happy with the shape, wrap the whole dog with needlepunch felt.

6 Cut out spots from the black needlefelt. Card or brush the white merino roving. Wrap the carded merino roving all around the dog's body. Use a felting needle to punch the fibers into all the creases and crevices.

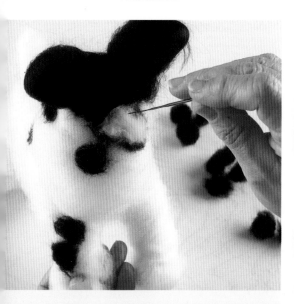

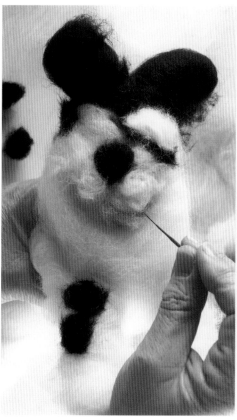

7 Wrap black merino fibers over and around the ears. Position black needlefelt spots on the dog, using a felting needle. Use one spot for the nose and three to make a patch in the eye position. Cover part of the patch with white merino fibers to create a ring of black.

8 Cut a mouth from the piece of pink needlefelt and needle this into place, with a felting needle. Cover part of the pink area with some white merino fibers, to make the dog's muzzle. When you are happy with the arrangement of patches, wet felt the dog following Steps 8–11 of Groovy Cat on pages 62–63. When the dog has dried, stitch the eyes in position, using black thread.

Sausage Dog

This dachshund is adapted from the Basic Animal Skeleton. It resembles the Spotty Dog, but it has a longer body, shorter legs, and a longer head. One of my childhood friends had a sausage dog called Kimmy, who had a wonderful temperament and never once barked or bit us. We would dress him up in our dolls' clothes and he would patiently wait until we had gone out to play before wriggling out of the frilly dresses and bonnets.

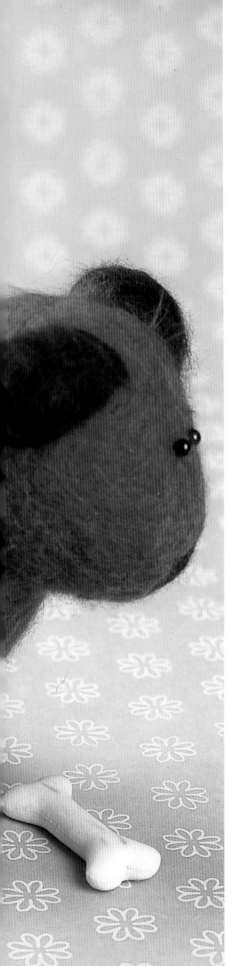

TOOLS AND MATERIALS

▸ **Basic Animal Skeleton from page 55**

▸ **Undyed merino needlepunch felt, 20 in./ 51 cm square, cut into ½ in./12 mm strips**

▸ **2 oz/50 g white cheviot roving**

▸ **Pair of wool carders or dog brushes**

▸ **Merino roving: 3½ oz/100 g dark brown, 3½ oz/100 g light brown**

▸ **Needlefelt in ⅓ oz/10 g black (see How to Make Needlefelt on page 20)**

▸ **Fabric scissors**

▸ **Felting needle**

▸ **Shallow tray**

▸ **1 piece of bubblewrap, large enough to line the tray**

▸ **Hot, soapy solution**

▸ **Plastic bowl**

▸ **Dishwashing brush**

▸ **Mesh laundry bag**

▸ **2 black glass beads**

▸ **Needle and black thread**

▸ **Finished size: 10¾ in./ 27 cm long x 6 in./15.5 cm high**

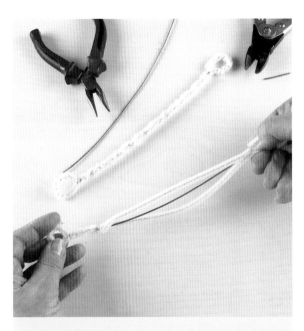

1 Make a pair of short legs for the dachshund by adjusting Steps 1–6 of the Basic Animal Skeleton. Begin by cutting 2 in./5 cm from the end of the two pipe cleaners in Step 1. Wrap the two pipe cleaners around a length of copper wire. Use more pipe cleaners if necessary to conceal the wire. Repeat to make the second pair of short legs.

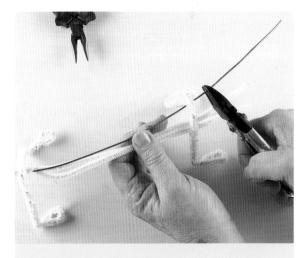

2 Make the dachshund's body by following Steps 7 and 8 of the Basic Animal Skeleton, but make the body 50 percent longer this time. Decide on the length by bending the two pairs of legs over the back of the body.

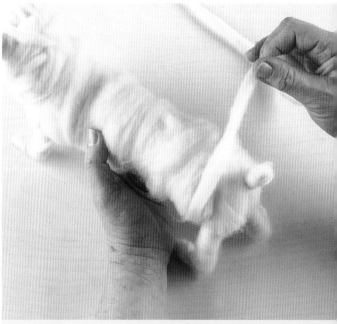

3 Make the head following Steps 11–14, but make it egg-shaped rather than ball-shaped. Cut a pipe cleaner in half to make ears and attach them to either side of the head. Use one quarter of a pipe cleaner to make a nose. Wrap the nose with needlepunch felt to emphasize its shape.

4 Wrap the body first with needlepunch felt and then with slivers of cheviot roving. Build up the underside of the body by adding layers of cheviot roving, then wrap the whole dog with needlepunch felt as shown.

5 Brush or card the merino roving. Wrap the ears, feet, and tail in dark brown merino fibers, making sure that there are no white patches showing through.

6 Wrap the whole body in light brown, making sure that you cross the fibers, as this will help the fibers to bond during the wet-felting process. Make sure that there are no white patches showing and that the ears and muzzle are well defined.

8 Cut out a triangular shape from the black merino needlefelt and fix the nose to the muzzle with a felting needle. When you are happy with the arrangement of patches, wet felt the dog following Steps 8–11 of Groovy Cat on pages 62–63. When the dog has dried, stitch the eyes in position, using black thread.

7 Use the felting needle to ensure the fibers stay in position.

To make a smart coat for the sausage dog, make some flat felt in your chosen color, using the coat pattern below. Measure your sausage dog to determine how big to make the coat. The felt will shrink by 30 to 35 percent, so make sure that the pattern is 30 to 35 percent larger than the finished size. Make a long piece of flat felt (see How to Make Flat Felt on page 16) in a contrasting color, to use as an edging for the coat. When the felt is dry, lay the pattern on top, and cut out the coat. Use the contrasting color to cut narrow strips for the edging. Cut two short pieces from one strip and attach these to the middle of both short edges of the coat, to form straps, then sew a button to one strap, and a small slit in the other, as a buttonhole.

Percy Pig

This little piggy uses the Basic Animal Skeleton from page 55, but has a longer tail, which can be curled up. To give the pig a fancy waistcoat, use the template on page 76. Use a long scrap of flat felt to make a bow tie.

TOOLS AND MATERIALS

▶ **Basic Animal Skeleton from page 55**

▶ **Approximately three 1 ft/30 cm pipe cleaners**

▶ **Flat-nosed pliers**

▶ **Undyed merino needlepunch felt, 20 in./51 cm square, cut into ½ in./12 mm strips**

▶ **2 oz/50 g white cheviot roving**

▶ **Pair of wool carders or dog brushes**

▶ **Merino roving: 3½ oz/100 g fawn, ⅓ oz/10 g pale pink**

▶ **Needlefelt in ⅓ oz/10 g pale pink (see How to Make Needlefelt on page 20)**

▶ **Fabric scissors**

▶ **Felting needle**

▶ **Shallow tray**

▶ **1 piece of bubblewrap, large enough to line the tray**

▶ **Hot, soapy solution**

▶ **Plastic bowl**

▶ **Dishwashing brush**

▶ **Mesh laundry bag**

▶ **2 black glass beads**

▶ **Needle and black thread**

▶ **Finished size: 8 in./20 cm long x 9¾ in./24.5 cm high**

1 Make the pig's head from three circles of pipe cleaners, following Steps 11–13 of the Basic Animal Skeleton on pages 57–58.

2 To make a snout for the pig, make a circle with one pipe cleaner by winding it around twice. Use the flat-nosed pliers to squeeze the ends of the pipe cleaner into the circle.

3 Wrap the snout circle with strips of needlepunch felt so the pipe cleaner is completely covered.

4 Cut one pipe cleaner in half and loop each half to make the ears. Fix one of these to each side of the head. Hold the wrapped snout circle to the front of the head and fix it to the head with a pipe cleaner cut into quarters. The head is now complete.

5 Cut a pipe cleaner into four pieces and use these pieces to fix the pig's head to the Basic Animal Skeleton on page 55. Wrap the ears, curly tail, and snout with strips of needlepunch felt.

6 Make the legs stout and solid by wrapping them with slivers of cheviot roving. Wrap the body, adding extra bulk around the pig's middle and neck. Use more slivers of roving to wrap the head, face, and snout.

Add color and felt the pig

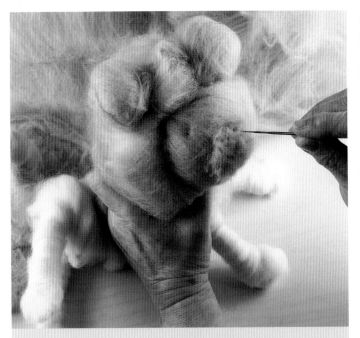

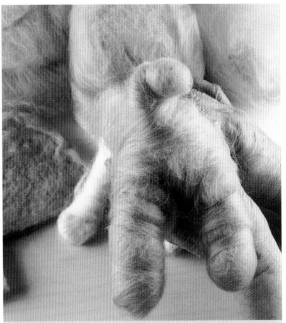

7 Prepare the fawn and pale pink merino fibers by carding or brushing. Wrap fawn fibers around the ears, head, and snout. Cut out a round shape from the pink needlefelt for the pig's nose. Fix the round shape in position on the front of the snout with a felting needle.

8 Wrap the legs and tail with the fawn fibers. Wrap some pink fibers to the end of the tail. Needle the fibers into all the creases and crevices with the felting needle so that none of the white needlepunch felt shows through.

9 Lay some pink fibers over the underside of the body and needle it into position. Continue to use the main color (fawn) for the rest of the pig. Tuck the fibers around the legs and neck, using the felting needle where necessary. Wet felt the pig following Steps 8–11 of Groovy Cat on pages 62–63. When the pig has dried, stitch the bead eyes in position, using black thread. Embroider nostrils on the snout, using more black thread.

This waistcoat template is shown here half actual size, and must be adapted to fit your finished pig. To make it, cut the waistcoat pattern from a piece of flat felt bearing in mind that the felt will shrink by 30 to 35 percent, so make sure that the pattern is 30 to 35 percent larger than the finished size. Make a long piece of multicolored flat felt (see How to Make Flat Felt on page 16). When the felt is dry, lay the pattern on top, and cut out the coat and the arm holes. Sew back the area around the neck to give the collar of the waistcoat some shape.

Funky Monkey

I love monkeys because they are so cheeky, and my particular favorite is the orangutan. This felted creature was inspired by orangutans and has been given a warm muffler made from a strip of multicolored flat felt. (See How to Make Flat Felt on page 16.)

TOOLS AND MATERIALS

- ▶ **Approximately twenty 1 ft/30 cm pipe cleaners**

- ▶ **Wire cutters**

- ▶ **Flat-nosed pliers**

- ▶ **1 ½ oz/40 g white cheviot roving**

- ▶ **Undyed needlepunch felt, cut into ½ in./12 mm strips**

- ▶ **Pair of wool carders or dog brushes**

- ▶ **Merino roving: ¾ oz/20 g pale pink, 2½ oz/60 g henna, small amount of shocking pink**

- ▶ **Needlefelt in ⅓ oz/10 g bright pink and ¾ oz/20 g pale pink (see How to Make Needlefelt on page 20)**

- ▶ **Fabric scissors**

- ▶ **Felting needle**

- ▶ **Shallow tray**

- ▶ **1 piece of bubblewrap, large enough to line the tray**

- ▶ **Hot, soapy solution**

- ▶ **Plastic bowl**

- ▶ **Dishwashing brush**

- ▶ **Mesh laundry bag**

- ▶ **2 black glass beads**

- ▶ **Needle and black thread**

- ▶ **FINISHED SIZE: 14 in./35.5 cm tall**

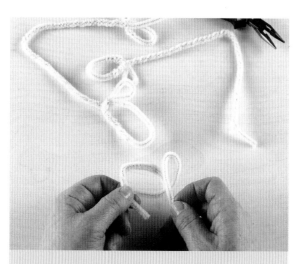

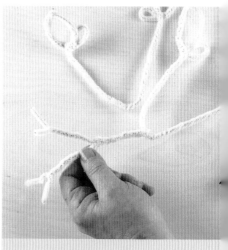

1 To make arms, twist two pipe cleaners together down their lengths, leaving tails at each end. Repeat the process with two more pipe cleaners then bend both twisted pieces in half. Make two loops in another pipe cleaner: one for the hand and a smaller one for the thumb. Repeat this to make a second hand. Make two feet, slightly larger than the hands. Attach the hands and feet to the arms and legs by bending over the loose tails.

2 To make the body, twist two pipe cleaners together. Fold this piece back on itself, catching the legs in the halfway position.

3 Attach the arms to the open ends of the body pipe cleaners and twist closed. Set aside the body for use in Step 5.

4 Make the monkey's head from three circles of pipe cleaners, following Steps 11–13 of the Basic Animal Skeleton on page 57–58. Attach two extra pipe cleaners to the base of the head to form a neck. Cut a pipe cleaner in half and use the pieces to make two ears; attach them to either side of the head.

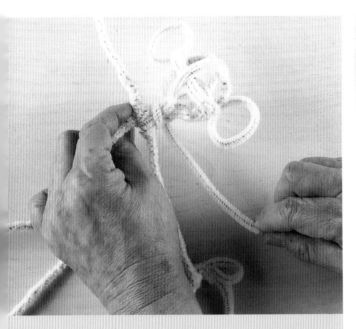

5 Attach the head to the body by wrapping another pipe cleaner around the neck where it meets the body.

6 Wrap pipe cleaners around the neck, and along the body to add strength. Use strips of needlepunch felt to wrap the hands and feet.

7 With cheviot roving, stuff the head cavity. Also wrap the body, arms, and legs.

8 Build up the body shape by wrapping the skeleton with plenty of cheviot roving. Build out the muzzle by wrapping some cheviot roving around your finger. Hold the roving in position on the face, then wrap it with needlepunch felt to hold it in place. When you are happy with the monkey's shape, wrap everything with needlepunch felt.

Add color and felt the monkey

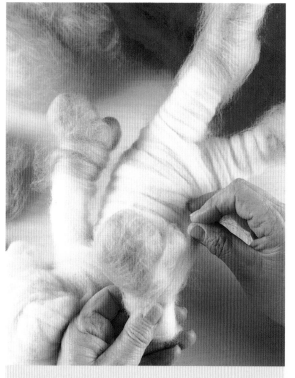

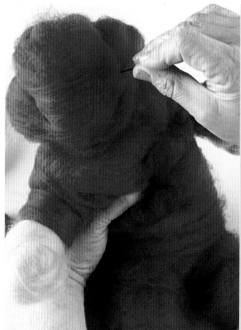

9 Brush or card the merino roving. Wrap the hands and feet in pale pink fibers, making sure that you cross the direction of the fibers whenever possible. Crossing the fibers will help the wet-felting process.

10 Wrap the body and head in henna fibers, making sure that each layer of fibers is perpendicular to the previous layer. Cover the body, head, ears, and between the legs with henna, but leave the hands and feet pink. Fix the fibers around the features with the felting needle so there is no white needlepunch felt showing through.

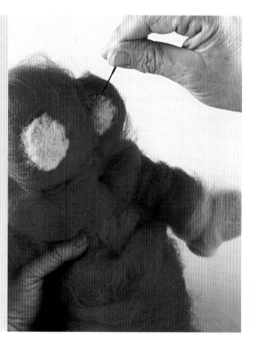

11 Cut a circle from the pale pink needlefelt for a muzzle, and two half circles for the insides of the ears. Needle these into place. Cut out a heart shape from bright pink needlepunch felt and a round patch for the monkey's butt. Fix these patches into position with a felting needle.

12 Wet felt the monkey following Steps 8–11 of Groovy Cat on pages 62–63. When the monkey has dried, stitch the bead eyes in position, using black thread. Embroider nostrils on the snout, using more black thread.

To make a chimpanzee instead of an orangutan, simply make the arms and legs shorter in Step 1 on page 78.

House Mouse

As a child, I adored Walt Disney's version of *Cinderella*. The scene I loved best was the one in which all the creatures help Cinderella spring-clean their home. The mice were so cute, with their little aprons and miniature brooms that they stayed in my imagination. Here is my version of a spring-cleaning mouse.

- ▶ Approximately twenty 1 ft/30 cm pipe cleaners

- ▶ 1ft/30 cm copper wire

- ▶ Wire cutters

- ▶ Flat-nosed pliers

- ▶ Undyed merino needlepunch felt, 24 in./ 61 cm square, cut into ½ in./12 mm strips

- ▶ 1½ oz/40 g white cheviot roving

- ▶ Pair of wool carders or dog brushes

- ▶ Merino roving: 2½ oz/60 g brown, small amount of black

- ▶ Needlefelt in ⅓ oz/10 g pale pink (see How to Make Needlefelt on page 20)

- ▶ Fabric scissors

- ▶ Felting needle

- ▶ Shallow tray

- ▶ 1 piece of bubblewrap, large enough to line the tray

- ▶ Hot, soapy solution

- ▶ Plastic bowl

- ▶ Dishwashing brush

- ▶ Mesh laundry bag

- ▶ 2 black glass beads

- ▶ Needle and black thread

- ▶ Colorless nylon fishing line

- ▶ FINISHED SIZE: 8 in./20.5 cm tall

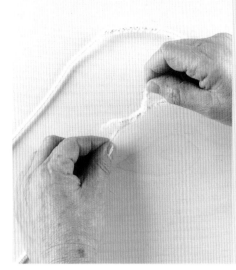

1 Join two pipe cleaners together to make a double length. Repeat this with two more pipe cleaners.

2 Twist the two double lengths together to make one thicker length. Leave tails at both ends. Set aside for use in Step 5.

3 Twist two pipe cleaners around the copper wire. Wrap along the length with another pipe cleaner to cover the wire completely.

4 Bend the piece you made in Step 3 into a semicircle. Wrap two slightly shorter pieces of pipe cleaners around another length of wire and cover with another pipe cleaner. Attach both sections together to make a reversed "D" shape.

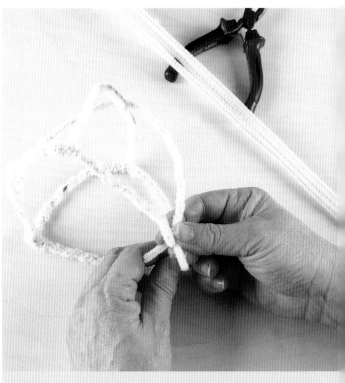

5 Take the double pipe cleaner length that you prepared in Steps 1 and 2. Attach this to either end of the straight side of the "D" to make an arch shape. Twist two pipe cleaners together and attach these to the top of the arch and the halfway point along the curve of the semicircle of the "D."

6 Make a bracing piece by twisting together two pipe cleaners and attaching these halfway up the frame.

7 Make a back foot for the mouse out of half a pipe cleaner, bent and twisted onto the straight edge of the "D." Repeat to make the second foot.

8 Make a paw with two-thirds of a pipe cleaner length. Bend the pipe cleaner in half, and twist to make arms, leaving a loop at the end for a paw. Attach both paws to the front of the frame.

9 Wrap the paws and feet in strips of needlepunch felt.

10 To create a face for the mouse, make a tripod by twisting six half pipe cleaners together to make three pieces joined to form a point. Attach the tripod by twisting the ends at three points over the front of the frame as shown.

11 To form an ear, cut a pipe cleaner in half and twist the two halves together. Attach the piece you have made to the side of the front frame. Squeeze in any sharp ends with the flat-nosed pliers. Repeat to make a second ear.

12 Use further pipe cleaners to form bracing pieces across the front of the frame.

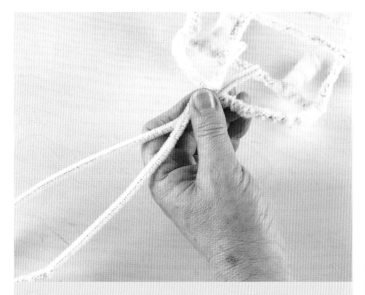

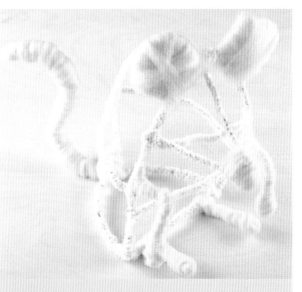

13 To make a tail, join two pipe cleaners together to make a long length. Fold this over and join the ends to the back of the body.

14 Wrap the nose, ears, and tail in needlepunch felt. Stuff the body cavity with loose cheviot roving. Wrap the body with slivers of cheviot roving then wrap the entire creature with needlepunch felt.

Add color and felt the mouse

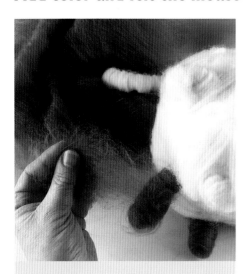

15 Card or brush the merino roving. Wrap the ears, feet, tail, and paws in mid brown merino fibers.

16 Wrap the nose with black merino fibers. Cut out two half circles of pink needlefelt for the insides of the ears. Cut another piece for the bib under the chin. Fix the needlefelt in position with a felting needle.

17 Wrap the body and the head in brown, and needle the fibers around the features, to ensure good coverage. Wet felt the mouse following Steps 8–11 of Groovy Cat on pages 62–63. Leave to dry.

18 Stitch black beads in place for the eyes, using a needle end black thread. To create whiskers, thread a needle with nylon thread. Push the needle through the head, from cheek to cheek.

19 Make a double knot with the nylon fishing line next to the left cheek. Pull hard on the nylon thread to create a knot tight against the right cheek. Double knot the thread again.

20 Repeat this process. If you wish, use a needle to create the knot, then slip the needle out and pull tight. Repeat the process to create an odd number of whiskers. (Odd numbers look best.) Trim the whiskers to approximately 2 in./5 cm.

This apron is made from a piece of flat felt that has been decorated with small squares of pre-felt. The apron ties are made from a long strip of flat felt.

Eight-legged skeletons can be adapted to make a range of multicolored creatures, both real and imaginary. A planet's worth of aliens look particularly attractive!

Eight-legged
Creatures

Basic Spider Skeleton

This is the basic skeleton for making any eight-legged creature. To create a tropical spider, I covered a red body with black and pink. Feel free to experiment with colors and patterns create a very handsome octopus or an alien from another world.

TOOLS AND MATERIALS

- Approximately twenty 1 ft/30 cm pipe cleaners
- 1 ft/30 cm copper wire
- Wire cutters
- FINISHED SIZE: 8 in./20.5 cm x 5½ in./14 cm

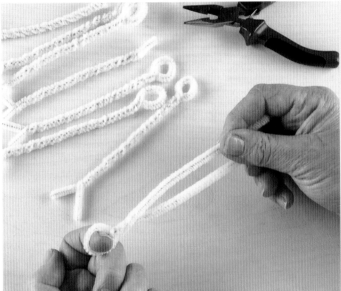

1 Fold a pipe cleaner in half. Place your finger in the fold then twist the two long halves of the pipe cleaner together to make a loop. Twist the two halves together down the length, leaving tails at the end. Repeat this seven times more to make eight legs.

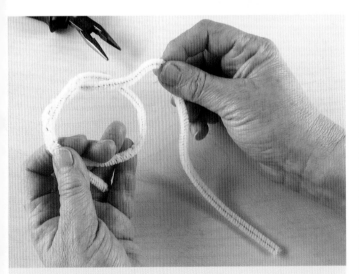

2 Join two pipe cleaners end-to-end to make a double length. Use this to make a large circle 3 in./7.5 cm in diameter. Twist in the ends and squeeze them flat with a pair of flat-nosed pliers.

3 Attach all eight legs to the circle one by one. Space the legs evenly around the circle. Use the tails from each leg to fix them to the circle.

4 Wrap the feet, the legs, and the circle with strips of needlepunch felt.

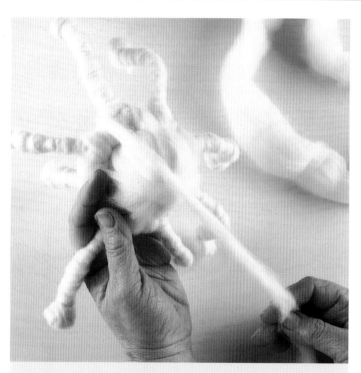

5 Make a ball from the cheviot roving and place it inside the circle to make the body. Wrap slivers of cheviot roving over the body and around the legs until you achieve the desired coverage.

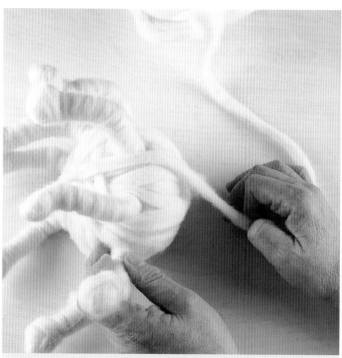

6 When you are happy with the body shape, wrap the body with strips of needlepunch felt.

Spotty Spider

Spotty Spider is built around the basic eight-legged skeleton, but is rather more colorful than the spiders you are likely to see around the woodpile!

TOOLS AND MATERIALS

- ► **Basic Spider Skeleton from page 89**
- ► **2 oz/50 g white cheviot roving**
- ► **Undyed needlepunch felt, 20 in./51 cm square, cut into ½ in./12 mm strips**
- ► **Pair of wool carders or dog brushes**
- ► **Merino roving: 1¼ oz/30 g pink, 2½ oz/60 g cherry red, handful of black**
- ► **Needlefelt in ⅓ oz/10 g black (see How to Make Needlefelt on page 20)**
- ► **Fabric scissors**
- ► **Felting needle**
- ► **Shallow tray**
- ► **1 piece of bubblewrap, large enough to line the tray**
- ► **Bamboo mat**
- ► **Hot, soapy solution**
- ► **Plastic bowl**
- ► **Dishwashing brush**
- ► **Mesh laundry bag**
- ► **2 black glass beads**
- ► **FINISHED SIZE: 8 in./20.5 cm x 5½ in./14 cm**

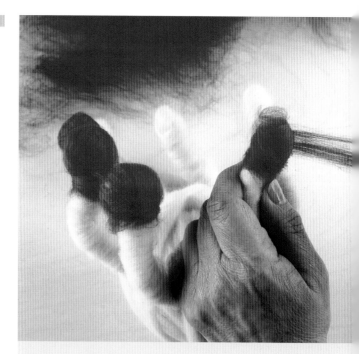

1 Card or brush the merino fibers. Wrap the feet with pink fibers, crossing the fibers as you layer the wool.

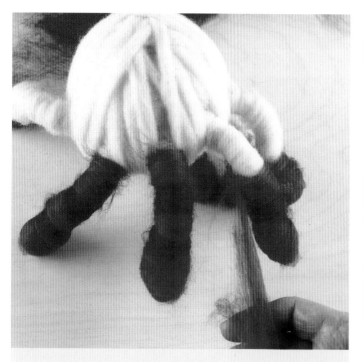

2 Use red fibers to wrap a little way up the leg. Continue to wrap the legs with pink, then red, to form stripes.

3 Cut out circles from the black needlefelt to use as spots on the spider's body. Start to wrap the body of the spider with red fibers. Laying the fibers in different directions will ensure a good, firm finish when the spider is wet felted.

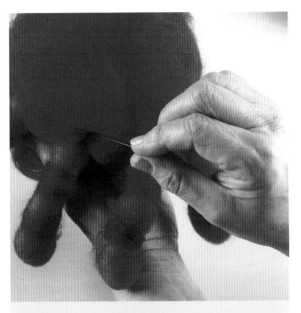

4 When you have finished wrapping the body and there is no white showing, fix the fibers around the tops of the legs with a felting needle.

5 Fix the black needlepunch spots in position around the top half of the body with a felting needle. Do not place them too close to each other as the wool shrinks as it felts and the gaps will be lost.

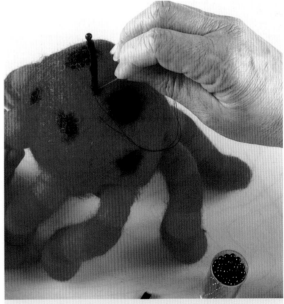

6 Wet felt the spider following Steps 8–11 of Groovy Cat on pages 62–63. Make black eye stalks from slivers of black merino fibers. Lightly wet the fibers with soapy solution and roll on a bamboo mat to make long, thin sausage shapes. Rinse these well and leave to dry, then cut into six pieces, each approximately 2 in./5 cm long.

7 Sew a black glass bead eye to each stalk (made in Step 9), then sew the eye stalks onto the body in a cluster.

VARIATIONS:
An Alien and an Octopus

Here are shown some of the variations possible on an eight-legged skeleton. To create an alien (opposite), make a black body and decorate it with circles cut from colorful oddments of flat felt. For a monster from the deep (below), give the basic creature a pink and red mouth made from flat felt. Attach this to the body with a felt stalk. The eye pods are felted rolls with black glass beads sewn on top. Spotty Spider (right) also has multiple eye stalks.

The Basic Hump-backed Skeleton is the basis for the Porcupine (page 99), the Dinosaur (page 104), and the Armadillo (page 111). The Dinosaur, in particular, can be customized with extra scales to make it as scary or amusing as you wish.

Hump-backed Creatures

Basic Hump-backed Skeleton

Following these instructions will give you a shell shape onto which details can added to make the characteristics of the different hump-backed animals.

TOOLS AND MATERIALS

▶ **Approximately twenty 1 ft/30 cm pipe cleaners**

▶ **1ft/30 cm copper wire**

▶ **Wire cutters**

▶ **Flat-nosed pliers**

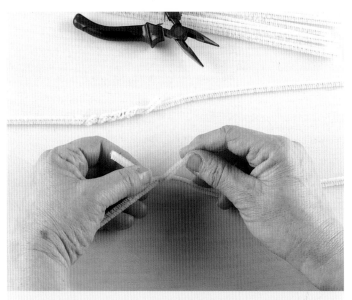

1 Twist two pipe cleaners together to make a long piece. Repeat to make a second long piece.

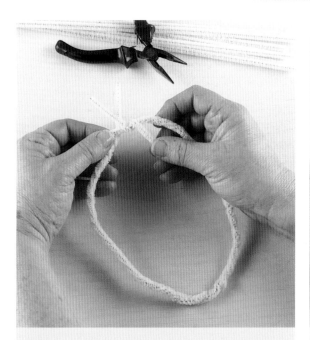

2 Twist the two long pieces together from Step 1 leaving the ends free. Loop this into a lemon shape: round at one end and pointed at the other. Twist the ends around the pointed end squeeze them flat with the pliers. Set aside.

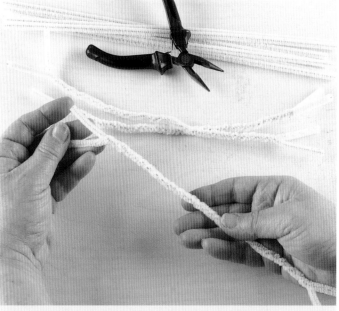

3 Twist two pipe cleaners together leaving the ends free. Repeat twice more to make three twisted struts. Set aside for use in Step 5.

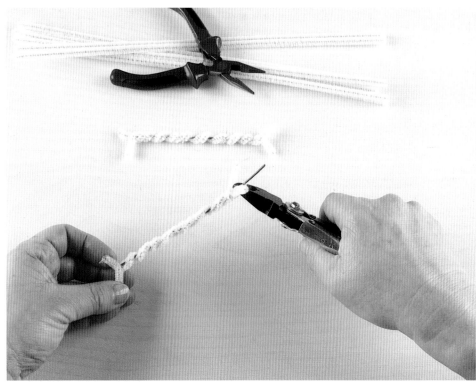

4 To make two strengthening straps, cut a pipe cleaner in half. Cut a piece of copper wire slightly shorter than half a pipe cleaner. Twist the two pipe cleaner halves over the copper wire leaving the ends of the pipe cleaner free as before. Trim the copper wire with the wire cutters. Repeat this to make a second strap.

5 Take the long struts made in Step 3. Run them from the pointed end of the lemon shape to the blunt end. Use the free ends of the struts to fix them to the frame. Fix the strengthening struts from Step 4 at right angles across the long struts. Use the free ends of the straps to fix them to the frame.

6 Cut two pipe cleaners into eight pieces with the wire cutter to use as ties over intersecting points on the shell.

Porcupine
Use the hump-backed skeleton shape to make the cutest porcupine ever. The colorful spines are made from scraps of merino fiber, sewn into the back of the porcupine.

- ▶ **Basic Hump-backed Skeleton from page 97**

- ▶ **Eight 1 ft/30 cm pipe cleaners**

- ▶ **Wire cutters**

- ▶ **Flat-nosed pliers**

- ▶ **8 in./20 cm copper wire**

- ▶ **1½ oz/30 g white cheviot roving**

- ▶ **Undyed merino needlepunch felt, 20 in./51 cm square, cut into ½ in./12 mm strips**

- ▶ **Pair of wool carders or dog brushes**

- ▶ **Dyed merino roving: 2½ oz/60 g dark brown, 1½ oz/30 g light brown, small amount of black**

- ▶ **Felting needle**

- ▶ **Shallow tray**

- ▶ **1 piece of bubblewrap, large enough to line the tray**

- ▶ **Hot, soapy solution**

- ▶ **Plastic bowl**

- ▶ **Dishwashing brush**

- ▶ **Mesh laundry bag**

- ▶ **Scraps of colored merino roving for the spines**

- ▶ **Blunt yarn needle**

- ▶ **Fabric scissors**

- ▶ **2 black glass beads**

- ▶ **Needle and black thread**

- ▶ **FINISHED SIZE: 7 in./18 cm x 5 in./13 cm**

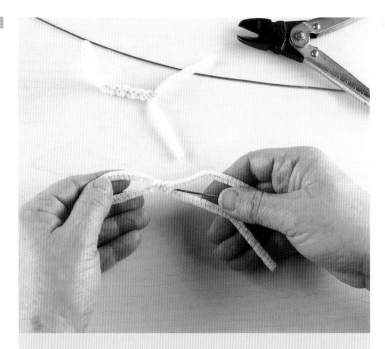

1 Fold a pipe cleaner in half. Twist the pipe cleaner at a point 1¼ in./3 cm from the fold, to make a foot. Enclose a 1½ in./3.75 cm length of copper wire to form the leg.

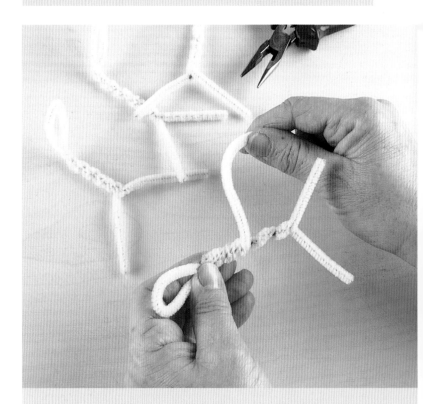

2 Wrap a pipe cleaner around the leg for added strength. Make three more legs in the same way.

3 Attach the four legs to the Basic Hump-backed Skeleton at the point where the bottom strengthening bars intersect.

4 Wrap the feet and legs in strips of needlepunch felt.

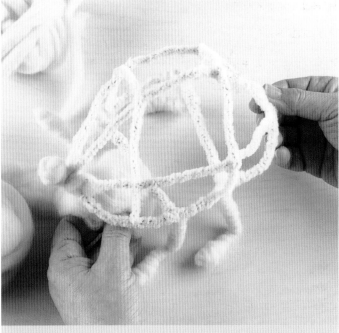

5 Make a nose by wrapping and knotting some strips of needlepunch felt. Leave the ends of the strips free and use these to attach the nose to the pointed end of the porcupine.

6 Stuff the head and body cavity with loose cheviot roving, making sure that the wool spills out of the open sides. This stuffing with shrink and harden in the felting process. Wrap the stuffed body with needlepunch felt.

Add color and felt the porcupine

7 Card or brush the merino roving. Use dark brown fibers to wrap the feet, legs, and nose, making sure that all the white areas are covered. Cross the directions of the fibers whenever possible.

8 Cover the body with light brown merino, once again making sure that no white shows through. Fix the fibers around the legs and nose with a felting needle.

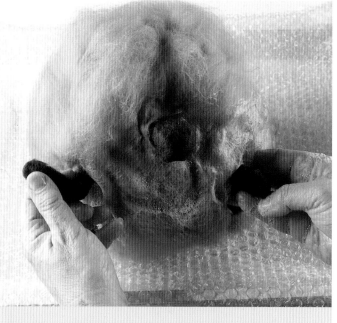

9 Begin to wet felt the porcupine following Steps 8–11 of Groovy Cat on pages 62–63. (Using a needle in Step 8 will encourage the colors to merge together.) On a large piece like this, it's important to work quickly so the hot, soapy solution does not have time to cool.

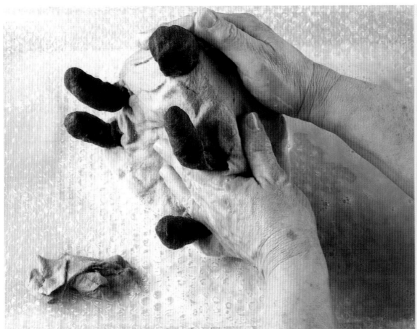

10 Massage the body all over, to encourage shrinkage. If there are any saggy areas, carefully cut off some of the excess before the fibers felt too much. Massage the legs, feet and nose. When the porcupine is thoroughly felted, rinse it well using very hot and cold water, alternately. Place in a wash bag and spin in a washing machine, the leave to dry.

11 When the porcupine is dry, make spines from dyed merino scraps. To make a spine, thread the yarn needle with a 3 in./7.5 cm length of colored merino. Working your way across the back of the porcupine, pinch the felt and push the needle through. Use pliers to grip and pull the needle through the felt, if necessary. Repeat with different colors all across the back of the porcupine. Wet the spines with hot, soapy solution and rub to part-felt them. Rinse very well and leave to dry.

12 Trim all the spines to the same length. To finish, pin the glass beads in position to make eyes, then sew them in place with a needle and black thread.

Dinosaur

The inspiration for this dinosaur came from watching the Flintstones on television as a child. I loved the way Fred Flintstone had to put Dino the dinosaur out at night with the empty milk bottles. Of course, this creature could just as easily be the Loch Ness Monster. Instructions for making the little felt cones in its head are on page 22.

TOOLS AND MATERIALS

▶ **Basic Hump-backed Skeleton from page 97**

▶ **Twelve 1 ft/30 cm pipe cleaners**

▶ **Wire cutters**

▶ **Flat-nosed pliers**

▶ **1½ oz/30 g of white cheviot roving**

▶ **Undyed merino needlepunch felt, 2ft/61 cm, cut into ½ in./12 mm strips**

▶ **Pair of wool carders or dog brushes**

▶ **Merino roving: ⅓ oz/10 g baby pink, 2½ oz/60 g bright blue, ¾ oz/20 g lime green, 2 oz/50 g blue-green**

▶ **Needlefelt in ⅓ oz/10 g blue-green (see How to Make Needlefelt on page 20)**

▶ **Fabric scissors**

▶ **Felting needle**

▶ **Shallow tray**

▶ **1 piece of bubblewrap, large enough to line the tray**

▶ **Hot, soapy solution**

▶ **Plastic bowl**

▶ **Dishwashing brush**

▶ **Mesh laundry bag**

▶ **Bamboo mat**

▶ **2 black glass beads**

▶ **Needle and black thread**

▶ **Finished size: 10 in./25.5 cm high x 14 in./35.5 cm long**

1 Take two pipe cleaners and twist them together to make one long wire. Make a second one. Bend each long length in half and secure them in the center with a pipe cleaner cut into quarters. This makes a tall pyramid shape.

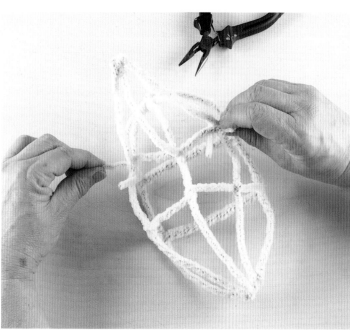

2 Create the dinosaur's tail by attaching the pyramid shape from Step 1 to the rounded end of the Basic Hump-backed Skeleton (the end without a join).

3 To make the neck, twist two pipe cleaners together leaving the ends free. Cut another pipe cleaner in half and twist these halves ends together leaving the ends free. Fold the long twisted pipe cleaners in half and attach the twisted half length to the center point to make a pyramid shape.

4 Attach the neck to the body at the pointed end. Attach the neck to the both sides of the shell and it in the middle of the back.

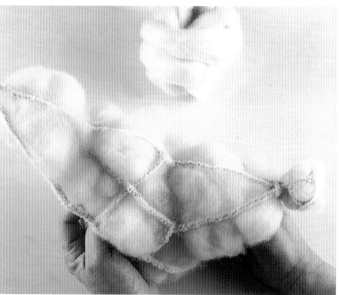

5 Make a head shape by following Steps 11–14 of the Basic Animal Skeleton on page 55. Use the loose tails to fix the head to the neck of the dinosaur.

6 Stuff the body and head cavity with plenty of loose cheviot roving, making sure that the wool spills out of the open sides.

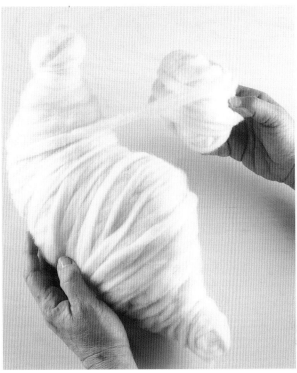

8 When you are happy with the shape of your dinosaur, wrap the whole creature with strips of needlepunch felt.

7 Wrap the stuffed head and body with slivers of cheviot roving.

Add color to the dinosaur

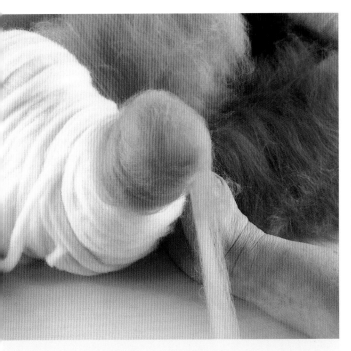

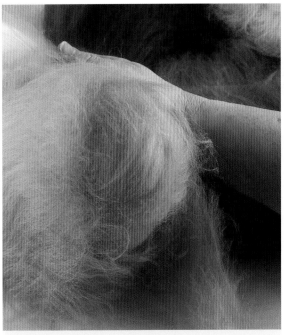

9 Card or brush the merino roving, and leave in separate color piles. Wrap the head, face, and neck with pink fibers, laying them in different directions so that the fibers cross each other.

10 Cross the bright blue merino fibers to help the felt to bond. Cover the whole body and wrap it around the head, like a headscarf, with the pink fibers peeping out.

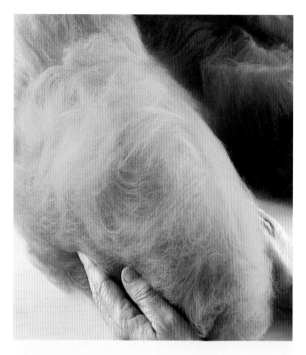

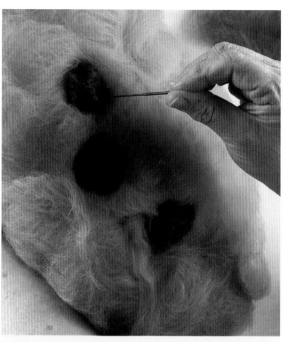

11 Lay lime green fibers in different directions over the spine of the dinosaur, like a saddle.

12 Cut out circles from the emerald green merino fibers and to make scales. Use the felting needle to attach them to the dinosaur's flanks, below the saddle area.

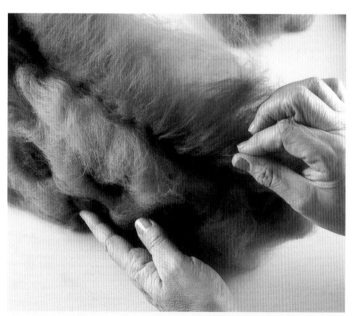

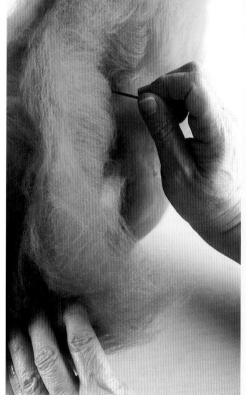

14 Lay some more blue-green between these two flaps, extending to the tip of the tail. Make sure that all the fibers are laid at right angles to the layer below.

13 Lay a long section of blue-green fibers along the spine. Needle this in place so that there are two flaps, one on either side of the body, and allow them to meet in the middle.

15 Begin to wet felt the dinosaur following Steps 8–11 of Groovy Cat on pages 62–63. Working quickly so the soapy solution stays hot, will encourage the wool to felt. Rub well, starting at the head.

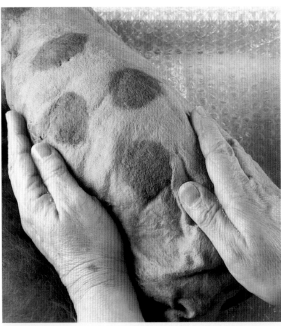

16 Massage the entire body, concentrating on felting and hardening the fibers on the dinosaur's flanks.

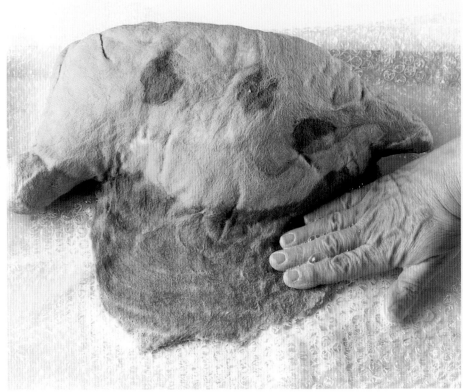

17 Make sure the needlefelt spots felt into the body. Rub the spine repeatedly against a bamboo mat to harden and stiffen it.

18 Rinse well by immersing the dinosaur alternately in very hot water then cold water. While the felt is still wet, cut the back spine and rub the edges to stiffen it. Put the dinosaur into a wash bag and spin in a washing machine. Remove from the bag and leave to dry naturally.

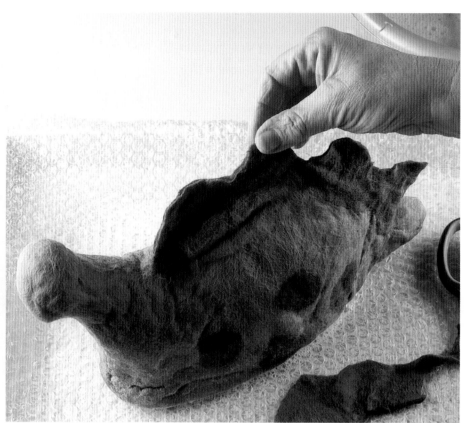

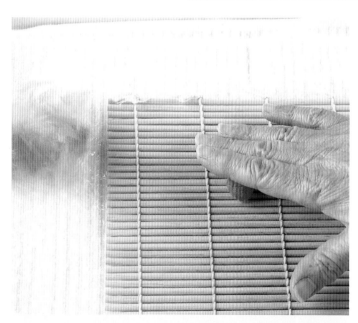

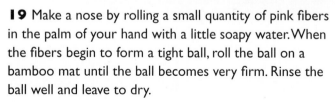

19 Make a nose by rolling a small quantity of pink fibers in the palm of your hand with a little soapy water. When the fibers begin to form a tight ball, roll the ball on a bamboo mat until the ball becomes very firm. Rinse the ball well and leave to dry.

20 When the dinosaur is dry, decorate the head and back of the neck with felt cones. When the nose is dry, stitch it in place. Use black thread to stitch a mouth, then stitch the eyes in position.

Armadillo

This Armadillo is a tribute to the hairy armadillo that I used to visit once a week at London Zoo, when I worked there as a volunteer. My tour of duty was never complete without a visit to my friend. I always wondered how he got his name, as clearly he was not hairy, apart from a little fringe around his body. The basis of this armadillo is the Basic Hump-backed Skeleton from page 97.

TOOLS AND MATERIALS

- Basic Hump-backed Skeleton from page 97

- Eight 1 ft/30 cm pipe cleaners

- Wire cutters

- Flat-nosed pliers

- 1½ in./40 g white cheviot roving

- Undyed merino needlepunch felt, 20 in./51 cm square, cut into ½ in./12 mm strips

- Pair of wool carders or dog brushes

- Merino roving: 2½ oz/60 g light mulberry, 1¼ oz/30 g pale pink, 1¼ oz/30 g deep mulberry, small amount of deep mauve

- Needlefelt in ¾ oz/20 g chestnut and ⅓ oz/10 g deep mulberry (see How to Make Needlefelt on page 20)

- Fabric scissors

- Felting needle

- Shallow tray

- 1 piece of bubblewrap, large enough to line the tray

- Bamboo mat

- Hot, soapy solution

- Plastic bowl

- Dishwashing brush

- Mesh laundry bag

- 2 black glass beads

- Needle and black thread

- Finished size: 5 in./13 cm high x 14 in./35.5 cm long

1 Prepare the nose by taking two pipe cleaners and twisting them together to make a long length. Bend each long length in half and secure in the center with a pipe cleaner cut into quarters.

2 Fix the nose extension to the pointed end of the Basic Hump-backed Skeleton. Fix two ends of the nose piece to either side of the join. Fix the other two ends to the body struts, going over and across the shell.

3 Wrap the nose point with slivers of cheviot roving, to make it wide and flat.

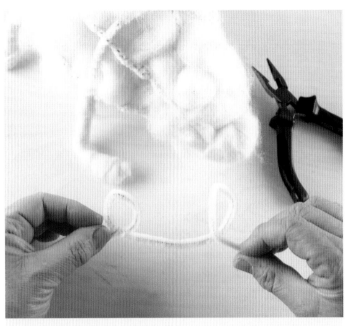

4 Stuff the skeleton with loose cheviot roving, making sure that the wool spills out of the open sides. This stuffing will shrink and harden in the felting process. Make ears by creating two loops in a pipe cleaner.

5 Position the ears on the top of the head and use the ends of the pipe cleaner to fix them in place.

6 Wrap the ears with slivers of cheviot roving. Wrap the whole body with cheviot roving and finish with a layer of wrapped strips of needlepunch felt.

Add color and felt the armadillo

7 Card or brush the merino fibers. Wrap the feet with pink merino, making sure that there are no white patches showing through. Cross the fibers often as you layer the wool.

8 Use the light mulberry fibers to wrap the ears, head, body, and underbelly, making sure that the fibers are laid crosswise. Extend the fibers beyond the back of the armadillo, to create a tail. Lay the fibers from the belly to the tail, crossing them around the tail.

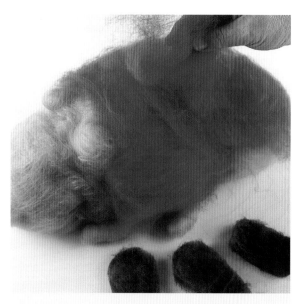

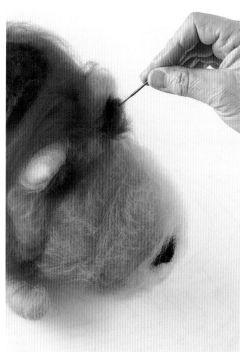

10 Lay the rectangular patches along the armadillo's back and tail, leaving equal spaces between the patches. Fix them in position with a felting needle. Cut a triangular snout from the chestnut needlefelt, lay it in position, and needle it into the fibers. Fix some mauve merino fibers inside the ears with the felting needle.

9 Lay the deep mulberry merino fibers over the back and the top of the tail, ending just behind the ears. Cut the chestnut needlefelt into three rectangles and a triangle for the armadillo's snout.

11 Wet felt the armadillo following Steps 8–11 of Groovy Cat on pages 62–63. Cut slits into the mulberry needlefelt to make fringes. Wet felt this into the body, but keep the fringes separate so they don't matt together too much. Rinse well and leave to dry. Position the eyes, then stitch them in place with a needle and black thread.

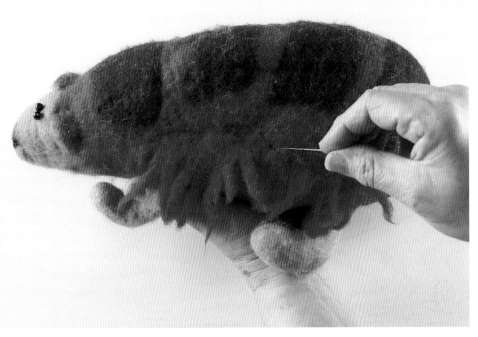

After making a selection of felt critters, you are likely to be left with leftover wool fibers and pipe cleaners. These can be put to good use by turning them into simple projects that children can make with a little adult supervision. The methods used to create the spider and butterfly mobiles can be adapted to make mobiles using other creatures. Why not make a bat mobile for a Halloween party?

Using Up

Scraps

Butterfly Mobile
Butterflies are ideal subjects for a mobile and are perfect for using up scraps of merino fibers. A multicolored collection of butterflies makes an attractive feature to hang over a baby's cot or to suspend in front of a sunny window.

TOOLS AND MATERIALS

▶ **4 white 1 ft/30 cm pipe cleaners per butterfly**

▶ **Flat-nosed pliers**

▶ **Merino roving: small handfuls of bright colors**

▶ **⅓ in./9 mm/ wooden dowel, 2 ft/61 cm long**

▶ **Needle and strong black thread**

▶ **Small hacksaw**

▶ **Pencil**

▶ **Ruler**

▶ **Scissors**

▶ **FINISHED SIZE: 4 in./10 cm x 3 ½ in./9 cm**

Children can easily make these butterflies, although they will need adult assistance with the pliers and the construction of the mobile. Once the butterflies have been wrapped in fibers, you may wish to customize the butterflies with dots made from needlefelt off-cuts. Simply stick these in place with dabs of fabric glue.

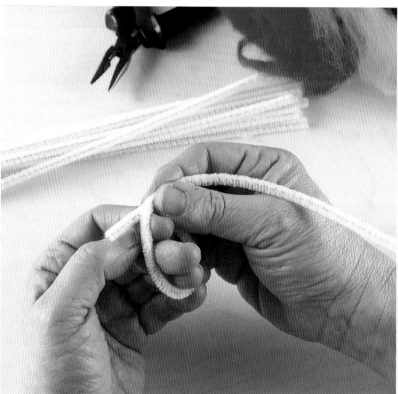

1 To make the top section of a butterfly's wing, wind one end of a pipe cleaner around three fingers. (Wind it around the whole hand, if it is a child who is making the butterfly.) Twist the loose end around the wing shape twice. Use the flat-nosed pliers to smooth the ends.

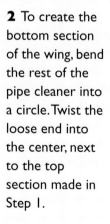

2 To create the bottom section of the wing, bend the rest of the pipe cleaner into a circle. Twist the loose end into the center, next to the top section made in Step 1.

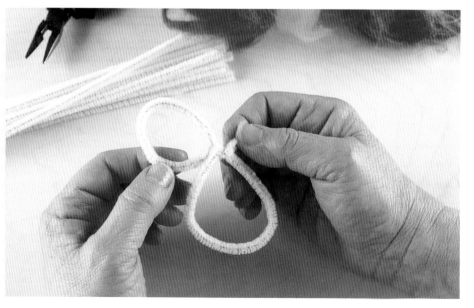

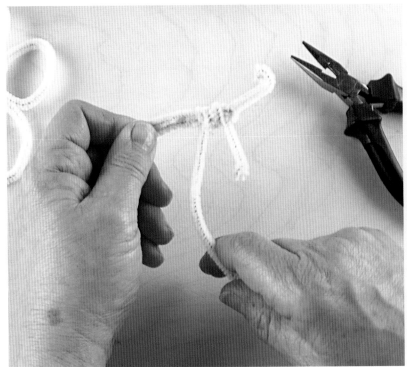

3 Repeat Steps 1 and 2 to make a second wing. Make the body of the butterfly by folding a pipe cleaner in half. Leave the 1 in./2.5 cm free at the end, and fold in half again. (The free ends will form the antennae.) Wrap another pipe cleaner around the body in a spiral, then use the pliers to curl the ends of the antennae.

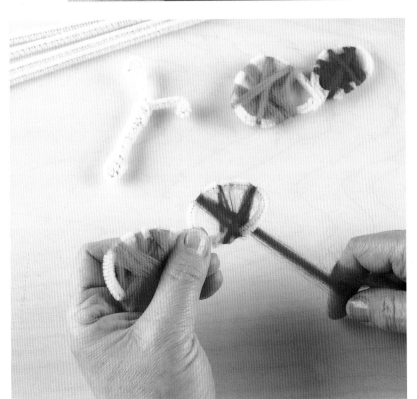

4 Wrap slivers of brightly colored merino fiber around the top and bottom sections of each wing in a crisscross pattern.

5 Use a different color to cover the body, wrapping all the way up to the antennae, and crossing the fibers as you proceed.

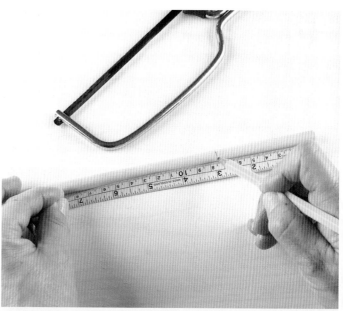

6 Lay the butterfly on the work surface, with the body in the center. Use a sliver of fiber to wrap the body and wings together across the center space between the top and bottom sections of the wings.

7 Make another six butterflies, each in a different color combination. Use the pencil to mark 2 in./5 cm from either end of the dowel, then divide the remaining length into six equal parts.

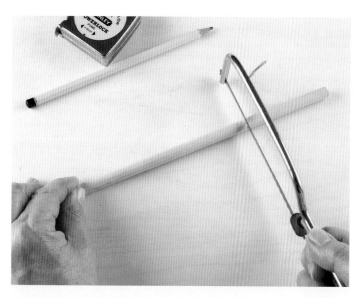

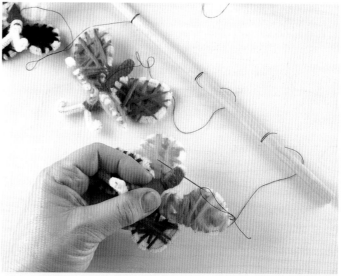

8 Make a shallow cut with the hacksaw on each pencil mark along the wooden dowel.

9 Tie a 30 in./76 cm length of thread around each saw cut, leaving the ends hanging. Thread a needle onto each end in turn and stitch through the body of a butterfly. Secure with a knot, adjusting the thread so that the butterflies hang at different heights. Tie the ends of a length of thread to each end of the dowel, so the mobile can be hung.

Spider Mobile

These spiders are simple enough for children to make and cute enough to win the hearts of arachnophobes everywhere. With a little help from an adult, the spiders can be turned into a mobile. Make seven small spiders, each with different, brightly colored abdomens and ankle socks.

- 8 black 1 ft/30 cm pipe cleaners per spider

- Merino roving in two bright colors per spider

- Flat-nosed pliers

- ⅓ in./9 mm/wooden dowel, 2ft/61 cm long

- Small hacksaw

- Pencil

- Tape measure

- Scissors

- Sewing needle and black thread

- Craft glue

- Finished size: 4 in./10 cm x 4 in./10 cm

1 To make the legs, cut two pipe cleaners in half. Hold the end of the four halves in one hand and wrap half a pipe cleaner around the middle of the pipe cleaners with the other. Twist to hold in place. The spider will now have eight legs and two antennae.

2 Spread out the eight legs. Take a sliver of brightly coloured merino fiber and wrap it around the middle.

3 Wrap the fiber between each of the legs then back over the body to form a fat abdomen.

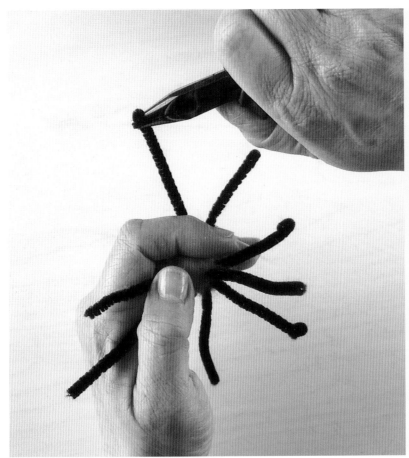

4 Form a foot at the end of each leg by bending back the tip of the pipe cleaner with the flat-nosed pliers.

5 Wrap a sliver of a different color merino fiber around each leg of the spider, to make socks.

6 Use the pliers to curl the ends of the pipe cleaner used to wrap the legs in Step 1, to finish the antennae. Make another six spiders.

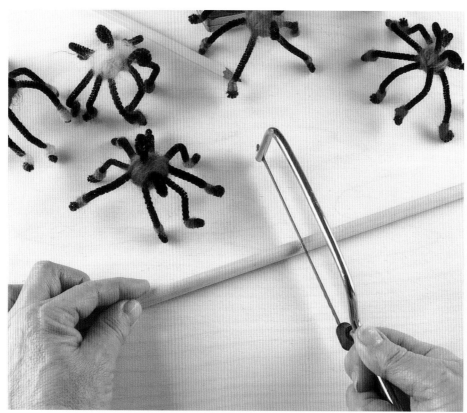

7 Use the pencil to mark 2 in./5 cm from either end of the dowel, then divide the remaining length into six equal parts. Make a shallow cut with the hacksaw on each pencil mark.

8 Tie a 30 in./76 cm length of thread around each saw cut, leaving the ends hanging. Thread a needle onto each end in turn and stitch through the colored abdomen of a spider. Secure with a knot, adjusting the thread so that the butterflies hang at different heights. Tie the ends of a length of thread to each end of the dowel, so the mobile can be suspended.

Suppliers

Blacksheep Designs
518-797-5191
www.blacksheepdesigns.com
Felting supplies, tools, kits, books, and videos

Cartwright's Sequins
www.ccartwright.com
Glitter, sequins, buttons, and beads

Craft Supplies for Less, Inc.
888-882-7238
www.craftsuppliesforless.com
Pipe cleaners

FeltCrafts
800-450-2723
www.feltcrafts.com
Felting supplies

Fine Fiber Press & Studio
541-917-3251
www.peak.org/~spark/fine.html
Felt making tools, equipment, and materials, fiber, prefelt, books, and classes

Friends Fiber Art
978-458-4200
www.friendsfabricart.com
Angelina, cotton, and silk fibers

Heirlooms Forever
800-840-4275
www.sews.com
Buttons, ribbon, threads, and floss

Lisa Souza Knitwear and Dyeworks
925-283-4058
www.lisaknit.com
Luxury hand-dyed fiber blends

Lori Flood Felted Fibers
The Spinster's Treadle
304-284-0774
www.spinsterstreadle.com
Felting fibers, felting supplies, and felting soap

Magpie Designs Felting Studio
413-256-6031
www.magpiefelt.com
Classes

Manny's Millinery Supply Co.
212-840-2235
www.mannys-millinery.com
Ribbon and wire

Metalliferous
888-944-0909
www.metalliferous.com
Wires and tools

Miriam Carter
603-563-8046
mcater@cheshire.net
Merino batts

New England Felting Supply
413-527-1188
www.feltingsupply.com
Merino and Norwegian batts, dyed prefelts, hand-dyed silks, local fleece and classes

Outback Fibers
800-276-5015
www.outbackfibers.com
Prefelts, silks, kits, batts, fibers, roving, and workshops

Paramount Wire Company
973-672-0500
www.parawire.com
Craft wire

R.H. Lindsay Co.
617-288-1155
www.rhlindsaywool.com
White merino top and other natural colored wools

Spirit Trail
703-309-3199
www.spirit-trail.net
Exotic and rare breed fibers

Susan's Fiber Shop
888-603-4237
www.susansfibershop.com
Glitz, cotton, silk, wool, and other fibers

Tandy Leather Factory
800-433-3201
www.tandyleatherfactory.com
Leather lacing and stitching

Threads and Notions
604-524-1955
www.threads-and-notions.com
Threads and buttons

Woodland Woolworks
800-547-3725
www.woodlandwoolworks.com
Felting needles

Credits

Putting together a book like this has to be a collaborative effort from the first ideas to the final notes, so many thanks go to Janet, Paula, and Jane at Breslich & Foss (especially Janet without whom this book would never have happened), not forgetting Shona and her lovely lunches. Also thanks to Patrick Neale and Polly Jaffe at The Bookshop, Chipping Norton, who encouraged me when my confidence was lacking and whose advice was particularly useful. Big thanks to my daughter Gemma, whose design talents I always look to, and my son Dan, who I bored and probably still bore with constant references to "the bookie." Thanks also to my good friend and neighbor Becky, who was always there to listen to my frustrations and the latest episode in the book writing saga, and to Mary for our regular coffee and chat times. And thanks to the best one of all, my wonderfully supportive and dear husband Ray, who must be thoroughly sick of felt and felt animals by now.

Breslich & Foss would like to thank the following individuals for their help in the creation of this book: editorial assistance, Jane Birch; design, Roger Daniels and Martin Hendry; project management, Janet Ravenscroft; photography, Shona Wood.

To see more of Sue Pearl's work, visit her website on *www.feltbetter.com*